THE COMPLETE POWER PRESSURE COOKER XL COOKBOOK

Karen Benett

Warning-Disclaimer

The purpose of this book is to educate and entertain. The author or publisher does not guarantee that anyone following the techniques, suggestions, tips, ideas, or strategies will become successful. The author and publisher shall have neither liability or responsibility to anyone with respect to any loss or damage caused, or alleged to be caused, directly or indirectly by the information contained in this book.

CONTENTS

INTRODUCTION

If you're thinking about making the leap from good to great, consider trying the Power Pressure Cooker XL. This revolutionary kitchen gadget is a highly efficient, modern-day invention that performs various cooking functions such as steaming, rice cooking, slow cooking, sautéing, and so forth. The Power Pressure Cooker XL utilizes the pressure of super-heated steam to cook your favorite meals.

Our time is precious and the last thing we want to do after a hectic day is to spend too much time in the kitchen, cooking and cleaning up. Moreover, there are specific kitchen skills every home chef should know. Is it worth it? The fact is that cooking amazing homemade meals does not require special culinary skills. It doesn't require a lot of time either. The answer is – choose a multipurpose kitchen appliance.

Everyone needs the Power Pressure Cooker XL, especially elderly people who love "set-it-and-forget-it" advantage, busy moms who might be distracted by their kids, and other busy people who are trying to find more time for leisure activities.

In a nutshell, the Power Pressure Cooker XL is an electric multi-cooker that is easy to use and energy-efficient: it saves your time, money and effort, while providing better-tasting food. It's just that simple!

THINGS YOU NEED TO KNOW BEFORE USING THE POWER PRESSURE COOKER XL

The whole cooking process in the Power Pressure cooker XL is easy to follow. You just plug it in, throw in your food, place the lid on your cooker, choose the desired function, and go about your business. However, regardless of this simplicity, there are several rules to bear in mind that can help you make the most of this latest generation technology. Here are six major points to keep in mind:

1. First things first: never use the Power Pressure cooker XL until you have read the manufacturer's manual thoroughly!

2. Make sure to cut your ingredients into pieces of an approximately equal size to enable them to cook evenly.

3. Do not force the cooker's lid open. When the pressure is completely released, carefully remove the lid.

4. Never fill the Power Pressure Cooker XL more than two-thirds full with food.

5. If you tend to adapt traditional recipes to your Power Pressure Cooker XL, add less liquid but more seasonings. Pressure cooking time may be adjusted to your personal preference.

6. When it comes to frozen foods, it is not necessary to defrost them before pressure cooking. Just remember to add an extra ten minutes of cooking time.

At first glance, you will notice a control panel with a lot of buttons. All you have to do is choose one of the pre-set buttons. But which one? This intelligent cooking machine can perform various advanced tasks. These are common functions:

KEEP WARM/CANCEL – with this fully automated function you can keep your food warm at the right temperature.

COOK TIME SELECTOR – this button enables you to select a specific time range.

TINE ADJUSTMENT – this function is very useful when you want to increase the pre-programmed time.

SLOW COOK – this program is so economical to use because it is great for cooking cheaper cuts, beans, and root vegetables. It is an excellent choice for everyone who wants a warm meal ready when they arrive home.

The other highly beneficial functions are MEAT/CHICKEN, BEANS/LENTILS, RICE/RISOTTO, SOUP/STEW, and CANNING/PRESERVING.

THE BENEFITS OF COOKING WITH YOUR POWER PRESSURE COOKER XL

The Power Pressure Cooker XL is known for its efficiency, ease of use, high standards and hygiene. Once you master the basics, cooking in your Power Pressure Cooker XL becomes a cinch. Here are just a few benefits of this programmable multi-cooker.

The Power Pressure Cooker XL can significantly cut cooking time and save energy.

You will be able to cook the complete meals to perfection in no time – 70% faster than traditional cooking methods like stovetop pots or a conventional oven. In addition, you can brown, sear and sauté food by using the inner pot before cooking under pressure. This "set-and-forget" cooking method allows you to save your time in the kitchen thanks to an air-tight lid that locks into place. Cooking liquids come to a boil under high pressure; they transform to a steam shortly thereafter. Consequently, the Power Pressure Cooker XL, your versatile, digital pressure cooker, is able to cook food more quickly than traditional appliances.

Did you know that pressure cookers became the most widely used household utensils during World War II? As a matter of fact, people needed to save fuel and cook inexpensive food. Simple!

It is obvious that quick cooking times mean less energy use. It is good for personal health and for Mother Earth.

The Power Pressure Cooker XL is a money saving kitchen gadget.

Customers have estimated that you can save hundreds of dollars a year with your Power Pressure Cooker XL. In addition, your Power Pressure Cooker XL will last 20 years or more!

The Power Pressure Cooker XL can cook almost everything, for inexpensive cuts of meat and root vegetables to sophisticated desserts and crowd-pleasing snacks. Even leftovers are made to look fantastic and taste delicious in your Power Pressure Cooker XL. This is the magic of one-pot cooking that will enchant you!

Healthy and flavorful meals.

Many studies have shown that pressure cooking tends to preserve valuable nutrients better than conventional methods such as grilling, frying, steaming, baking or boiling. A pressure cooking actually requires very little fat and water, so that your food retains most of its valuable nutrients. And guess what? The shorter cooking time will help you to cook great meals without nutrient loss.

Flavorful pasta, hearty stew, rich and luxurious dessert, deliciously gooey cake, slurp-worthy chicken soup... You don't necessarily need to give up these gorgeous dishes. You just have to make better food choices. The Power Pressure Cooker XL with its flavor infusion technology will help you find a good balance between indulgence and nutrition!

If you want to cook faster and eat better, but you are confused by all the information out there, this cookbook may help you. It contains 150 recipes with a lot of tasty cooking solutions that won't leave you indifferent! We are going to explore the surprising variety of great dishes you can make in your Power Pressure Cooker XL so you can happily indulge in a cooking experience!

POWER PRESSURE COOKER XLCOOKING GUIDE / SPECIFICATIONS

Please note that cooking times are approximate; use them as a guideline only. The Power Pressure Cooker XL requires the addition of liquid in some form. Never fill the inner pot of your Power Pressure Cooker XL above MAX line.

MEATS	Liquid / Cups	Cooking Time in Minutes
Beef/Veal, roast or brisket	3 – 4	35 – 40
Beef meatloaf	1	10 – 15
Beef, corned	4	50 – 60
Pork, roast	1	40 – 45
Pork, ribs	3	20
Leg of lamb	3	35 – 40
Chicken, whole	3 – 4	20
Chicken, pieces	3 – 4	15 – 20
Cornish hens	1	15

VEGETABLES	Liquid / Cups	Cooking Time in Minutes
Asparagus, whole	1	1 – 2
Beans, fava	1	4
Beans, green	1	2 – 3
Beans, lima	1	2
Beets	1	10
Broccoli	1	2
Brussel sprouts	1	4
Carrots, sliced	1	4
Corn on-the-cob	1	3
Pearl onions	1	2
Potatoes, chunks	1	6
Potatoes, whole	1	10 – 11
Squash, acorn	1	7
Squash, summer	1	4

SEAFOOD/FISH	Liquid / Cups	Cooking Time in Minutes
Clams	1	2 – 3
Lobster, whole	1	2 – 3
Shrimp	1	1 – 2
Fish, Soup, Stock	1 – 4	5 – 6

VEGETABLES & SIDE DISHES

1. Wheat Berry and Vegetable Breakfast

For this healthy breakfast, wheat berries are cooked gently and tossed with vegetables and Feat cheese – a winning combination!

Servings 6

Ready in about 30 minutes

NUTRITIONAL INFORMATION (Per Serving)

188 - Calories
10.3g - Fat
19.6g - Carbs
6.0g - Protein
2.7g - Sugars

Ingredients

- 4 ounces Feta cheese
- 1 cup cucumber, thinly sliced
- 1 ½ cups cherry tomatoes, halved
- 4 ½ cups water
- 2 teaspoons lemon rind, grated
- 1/2 cup red onions, chopped
- 2 ½ tablespoons grapeseed oil
- 1/2 teaspoon salt
- 2 cups dry wheat berries
- 1/2 teaspoon dried oregano
- 2 tablespoons balsamic vinegar

Directions

1. Press the "RICE/RISOTTO" key. Add the oil, wheat berries, water and salt to your Power Pressure Cooker XL; cook under HIGH pressure for 25 minutes.
2. Once the timer reaches 0, the cooker will automatically switch to "KEEP WARM". Press the "CANCEL" key. Switch the pressure release valve to open. When the steam is completely released, remove the lid.
3. Drain the wheat berries and rinse them through a colander. Place the wheat berries in a serving dish. Toss with the remaining ingredients. Serve chilled and enjoy.

2. Two-Mushroom Pâté

This mushroom spread is quick to prepare. You can use it to make a grab-and-go quick snack or an elegant party dinner.

Servings 16

**Ready in about
30 minutes
+ chilling time**

**NUTRITIONAL
INFORMATION
(Per Serving)**

39 - Calories
2.3g - Fat
3.0g - Carbs
1.6g - Protein
1.4g - Sugars

Ingredients
- 1/3 cup dry white wine
- 2 onions, peeled and sliced
- 1 ½ pounds fresh mushrooms, thinly sliced
- 1 ½ cups boiling water
- 1/2 teaspoon kosher salt
- 1/4 teaspoon black pepper, freshly cracked
- 1 cup dry mushrooms, rinsed
- 3 tablespoons butter

Directions
1. Press the "FISH/VEGETABLES/STEAM" key. In a heat-proof measuring cup, combine the dry mushrooms and boiling water. Cover and set aside. The mushrooms will soak up the water.
2. When your Power Pressure Cooker XL is hot, warm the butter. Now, sauté the onions until they're softened, about 5 minutes. Then, stir in the fresh mushrooms; sauté them until fragrant and golden brown, for 5 minutes longer.
3. Pour in the white wine; allow the wine to evaporate completely. Add the soaked mushrooms and stir to combine. Season with salt and pepper.
4. Close and lock the cooker's lid. Set the cooking time to 10 minutes. When the steam is completely released, remove the lid.
5. To make the pâté: mix the ingredients with an immersion blender for 5 minutes. Transfer to a refrigerator in order to chill completely before serving.

3. Sweet Potato Casserole with Marshmallows

Need more ideas for what to make with sweet potatoes?
You'll be eating this casserole all day long – for breakfast,
lunch, and dinner.

Servings 6

Ready in about
30 minutes

**NUTRITIONAL
INFORMATION
(Per Serving)**

39 - Calories
2.3g - Fat
3.0g - Carbs
1.6g - Protein
1.4g - Sugars

Ingredients

- 2 cups water
- 1/4 teaspoon freshly ground black pepper
- 1/2 teaspoon sea salt
- 1 teaspoon cayenne pepper
- 3 ½ pounds sweet potatoes, peeled and cut into quarters

For marshmallow-pecan topping:

- 1 cup brown sugar
- 1/3 cup walnuts, chopped
- 1/4 teaspoon freshly grated nutmeg
- 2 ½ tablespoons butter, melted
- 1/2 cup all-purpose flour
- 1 ¾ cups mini marshmallows

Directions

1. Press the "SOUP/STEW" key. Add the sweet potatoes, water, sea salt, cayenne pepper, and black pepper to the inner pot of your Power Pressure Cooker XL.
2. Lock the lid. Adjust the timer to 15 minutes.
3. When the steam is released, open your Power Pressure Cooker XL. Mash the cooked sweet potatoes; taste and adjust the seasonings if needed. Transfer this sweet potato puree to an oven-safe casserole dish.
4. Next, mix the flour, brown sugar, nutmeg, and butter to make the topping. Fold in the walnuts. Spread this topping mixture over the sweet potato puree. Top with mini marshmallows.
5. Bake at 400 degrees F in the preheated oven for 12 minutes. Enjoy!

4. Cheesy Broccoli Soup

Looking for creative ways to cook with broccoli? This silky soup is both healthy and gourmet. Enjoy!

Servings 6

Ready in about 40 minutes

NUTRITIONAL
INFORMATION
(Per Serving)

101 - Calories
4.1g - Fat
10.7g - Carbs
6.4g - Protein
4.1g - Sugars

Ingredients

- 2 ¾ cups vegetable broth
- 1/2 cup onions, chopped
- 1/2 cup parsnip, finely chopped
- 1 cup carrots, sliced
- 1 teaspoon paprika
- 1/4 cup ground black pepper, to taste
- 1 teaspoon salt
- 1 cup bell pepper, seeded and chopped
- 1 cup celery stalks, finely chopped
- 1/2 cup celery rib, finely chopped
- 2 cups broccoli, broken into small florets
- 1/2 cup Cheddar cheese, grated

Directions

1. Press the "SOUP/STEW" key. Place all of the above ingredients, except for the Cheddar cheese, in your Power Pressure Cooker XL.
2. Now, set the timer for 35 minutes. Place the lid on the Power Pressure Cooker XL.
3. Once the timer reaches 0, press the "CANCEL" key. Switch the pressure release valve to open. When the steam is completely released, carefully open your Power Pressure Cooker XL.
4. Puree the soup with an immersion blender. Serve the soup in individual bowls topped with the grated Cheddar cheese. Enjoy!

5. Winter Jalapeño Soup

Jalapeño pepper is a powerhouse of vitamins C and A.
Keep in mind that cooking decreases the heat of jalapeño
peppers. In this recipe, use crunchy and tangy pickled
jalapeño to enhance the flavor of your soup.

Servings 6

**Ready in about
45 minutes**

**NUTRITIONAL
INFORMATION
(Per Serving)**

150 - Calories
9.0g - Fat
12.8g - Carbs
4.7g - Protein
3.8g - Sugars

Ingredients

- 2 pickled jalapeño peppers, chopped
- 1/2 teaspoon ground cumin
- 1/2 teaspoon dried thyme
- 1 cup turnip, chopped
- 2 small-sized onions, finely chopped
- 1/2 stick butter, softened
- 1 cup parsnips, chopped
- 1 ½ cups carrots, chopped
- 1/2 cup celery stalk, chopped
- 1 quart chicken broth
- 4 ½ cups water
- 1 cup croutons, for garnish

Directions

1. Press the "SOUP/STEW" key and melt the butter for a minute or so. Then, add the celery, parsnips, turnip, carrots, onion and jalapeño; sauté the vegetables for about 6 minutes.
2. Add the rest of the above ingredients, except for the croutons. Seal the lid and set the timer for 35 minutes.
3. Once the timer reaches 0, press the "CANCEL" key. Switch the pressure release valve to open. Carefully remove the lid.
4. Ladle your soup into six individual bowls. Serve hot with croutons.

6. Smoky Red Lentil Soup

Red lentils are inexpensive and rich in protein, vitamin B, fiber, and iron. This stress-free lentil recipe may become a family favorite!

Servings 6

Ready in about 30 minutes

NUTRITIONAL INFORMATION (Per Serving)

317 - Calories
0.9g - Fat
58.1g - Carbs
20.3g - Protein
4.1g - Sugars

Ingredients

- 2 ¼ cups red lentils, rinsed
- 1/2 cup red bell pepper, seeded and coarsely chopped
- 2 pounds Yukon Gold potatoes, diced
- 1 bay leaf
- 1/2 teaspoon freshly ground black pepper, to taste
- 1 teaspoon salt
- 1/2 teaspoon smoked paprika
- 1 cup carrots, thinly sliced
- 1 cup onions, chopped
- 6 cups water
- 1 teaspoon minced garlic

Directions

1. Choose the "BEANS/LENTILS" function on the Power Pressure Cooker XL. Sauté the garlic, onions, paprika, bell pepper, carrots, potatoes, salt, black pepper for about 6 minutes; make sure to stir constantly.
2. Stir in the red lentils, bay leaves, and water.
3. Cover the pot and bring to HIGH pressure; cook for 20 minutes. Afterwards, use the quick-release method to release the pressure and remove the lid.
4. Taste and adjust the seasonings. Serve warm and enjoy!

7. Cauliflower Chowder with Velveeta Cheese

A rich and satisfying, this cheesy chowder is guaranteed to make your meals so much better. Serve this as a light lunch on a brisk and rainy autumn days.

Servings 8

Ready in about 20 minutes

NUTRITIONAL INFORMATION (Per Serving)

119 - Calories
6.4g - Fat
9.5g - Carbs
7.8g - Protein
4.5g - Sugars

Ingredients

- 2 ½ pounds cauliflower florets
- 1 teaspoon dried dill weed
- 1 shallot, chopped
- 1/2 teaspoon cumin powder
- 1/2 teaspoon ground black pepper, or more to your liking
- 1 teaspoon sea salt
- 1 ¼ cups Velveeta cheese
- 5 cups vegetable stock

Directions

1. Choose the "FISH/VEGETABLES/STEAM" function. Simply drop all the ingredients, except the cheese, in the Power Pressure Cooker XL.
2. Now, place the lid on, and set the cooking time to 10 minutes. Afterwards, remove the lid according to the manufacturer's directions.
3. Add the Velveeta cheese; stir until the Velveeta cheese is completely melted. Use your immersion blender to blend the soup for 3 minutes.

8. Creamed Summer Squash Soup

This soup recipe is sure to please vegans and vegetable lovers alike. In this recipe, you can substitute regular onions with the shallots and even Vidalia onions.

Servings 8

Ready in about 40 minutes

NUTRITIONAL INFORMATION (Per Serving)

120 - Calories
2.2g - Fat
19.6g - Carbs
7.9g - Protein
6.5g - Sugars

Ingredients

- 2 cups boiling water
- 1 cup bell peppers, diced
- 2 potatoes, diced
- 4 zucchinis, shredded
- 1/2 teaspoon paprika
- 1/2 teaspoon cumin powder
- 16 ounces silken tofu, pressed
- 2 cups vegetable stock
- 1 cup onions, peeled and chopped
- 2 pounds yellow summer squashes, shredded

Directions

1. Choose the "SOUP/STEW" function. Add the onions to your Power Pressure Cooker XL; then, sauté the onions until tender and translucent, about 5 minutes.
2. Add the remaining ingredients; place the lid on the Power Pressure Cooker XL and lock; cook for 30 minutes.
3. Remove the lid according to the manufacturer's directions. Allow it to cool before puréeing with an immersion blender.
4. Serve topped with freshly chopped parsley if desired. Enjoy!

9. Purple Cabbage and Apple Dinner

Amaze your family with this sweet and tart dinner. You can add a few drizzles of vinegar to lock in the fantastic purple color of your cabbage.

Servings 4

Ready in about 30 minutes

NUTRITIONAL INFORMATION (Per Serving)

157 - Calories
3.7g - Fat
24.0g - Carbs
2.6g - Protein
11.6g - Sugars

Ingredients

- 1 pound purple cabbage, shredded and stems removed
- 1/2 teaspoon brown sugar
- 1 ½ cups chicken stock
- 1/2 cup dry red wine
- 1 cup onions, diced
- 1/4 teaspoon allspice
- 1/2 teaspoon ground black pepper
- 1 teaspoon salt
- 1 teaspoon dried thyme
- 1 tablespoon lard, room temperature
- 1 cup tart apples, peeled, cored and diced
- 1 ½ tablespoons all-purpose flour
- 1 ½ tablespoons cornstarch dissolved in 6 teaspoons dry red wine

Directions

1. Choose the "FISH/VEGETABLES/STEAM" function on your Power Pressure Cooker XL. Warm the lard until it's completely melted.
2. Then, sauté the onions and apples until soft, about 7 minutes. Add the remaining ingredients, except the cornstarch slurry.
3. Dust with flour and give it a gentle stir. Set the cooking time to 15 minutes. Perform a quick-release and open the Power Pressure Cooker XL.
4. Next, press the "CHICKEN/MEAT" key and bring to a boil; add the prepared cornstarch slurry.
5. Then, boil for 4 minutes, uncovered, or until the cooking liquids have thickened. Serve warm.

10. Summer Wheat Berry Salad

Here's a million-dollar salad you will crave during summer days! Toss together these healthy and fresh ingredients and serve the best wheat berry salad ever!

Servings 6

Ready in about 30 minutes + chilling time

NUTRITIONAL INFORMATION (Per Serving)

218 - Calories
12.0g - Fat
21.4g - Carbs
9.1g - Protein
3.4g - Sugars

Ingredients

- 2 cups dry wheat berries
- 1 ½ cups cherry tomatoes, halved
- 1/2 cup red onions, chopped
- 3 tablespoons olive oil
- 1/2 teaspoon salt
- 1 teaspoon olive oil
- 2 tablespoons balsamic vinegar
- 2 ½ cups water
- 1/2 teaspoon dried oregano
- 2 sprigs dried rosemary
- 1/2 teaspoon orange rind, grated
- 1 cup red bell pepper, cut into strips
- 1/2 cup green bell pepper, cut into strips
- 4 ounces Mozzarella cheese
- 2 ½ cups vegetable stock

Directions

1. Press the "RICE/RISOTTO" key. Add 2 tablespoons of olive oil, wheat berries, water, vegetable stock and salt to your Power Pressure Cooker XL; cook for 25 minutes.
2. Once the timer reaches 0, the cooker will automatically switch to "KEEP WARM". Press the "CANCEL" key. Switch the pressure release valve to open. When the steam is completely released, remove the lid.
3. Drain the wheat berries and rinse them through a colander. Place the wheat berries in a serving bowl. Toss with the remaining ingredients. Serve chilled and enjoy

11. Spiced Vegetable Soup

This immunity-boosting soup is full of amazing, valuable nutrients. You can substitute chicken broth for a vegetable stock.

Servings 6

Ready in about 45 minutes

NUTRITIONAL INFORMATION (Per Serving)

134 - Calories
7.0g - Fat
14.2g - Carbs
4.7g - Protein
6.2g - Sugars

Ingredients

- 2 ½ tablespoons grapeseed oil, softened
- 1 quart chicken broth
- 1 cup celery stalk, chopped
- 4 ½ cups water
- 1/2 pound carrots, chopped
- 1 cup yellow bell pepper, seeded and chopped
- 1 cup red bell pepper, seeded and chopped
- 1/2 teaspoon fennel seeds
- 1 teaspoon celery seeds
- 1/4 teaspoon ground cumin
- 1 cup parsnips, chopped
- 1 cup leeks, finely chopped

Directions

1. Choose the "SOUP/STEW" function and warm the grape seed oil for a minute or so. Then, stir in the parsnips, bell peppers, carrots, celery and leek; sauté the vegetables for approximately 7 minutes.
2. Stir in the remaining ingredients. Place the lid on the Power Pressure Cooker XL and lock. Now, set the timer for 35 minutes.
3. When the steam is released completely, remove the lid. Serve hot and enjoy.

12. Lasagna with Mushrooms and Cottage Cheese

If you have never had a vegetarian lasagna in the Power Pressure Cooker XL, here is a great idea! Mushrooms can be a great source of protein so you don't need any meat for this delicious lasagna.

Servings 6

Ready in about 35 minutes

NUTRITIONAL INFORMATION (Per Serving)

578 - Calories
6.4g - Fat
99.0g - Carbs
30.4g - Protein
8.1g - Sugars

Ingredients

- 3 cloves garlic, minced
- 2 cups pasta sauce
- 2 cups Cottage cheese
- 2 sprigs dried rosemary
- 1 teaspoon red pepper flakes, crushed
- 1/2 teaspoon sea salt
- 1/2 teaspoon dried basil
- 1/2 teaspoon dried oregano
- 1/2 teaspoon ground black pepper
- 2 cups mushrooms, thinly sliced
- 2 pounds dry lasagna noodles

Directions

1. Choose the "FISH/VEGETABLES/STEAM" function. Treat a spring-form pan with a nonstick cooking spray.
2. Add the lasagna noodles to the bottom of the pan. Spread the pasta sauce. Lay the Cottage cheese.
3. Top with the sliced mushrooms. Sprinkle with some minced garlic, spices, and herbs. Repeat the layers until you run out of ingredients. Cover with an aluminum foil.
4. Next, place the wire rack on the bottom of your Power Pressure Cooker XL. Pour in 1 cup of water.
5. Lower the spring-form pan onto the wire rack; lock the cooker's lid and switch the pressure release valve to closed. Set the cooking time to 25 minutes.
6. Once the cooking is done, switch the pressure release valve to open. When the steam is completely released, remove the cooker's lid. Serve warm.

13. Colorful Brown Rice Salad

Looking for a last-minute recipe for a family dinner? This stunning rice salad will fit the bill! Wild rice works well in this recipe, too; just increase the cooking time to 25 minutes.

Servings 4

Ready in about 25 minutes + chilling time

NUTRITIONAL INFORMATION (Per Serving)

398 - Calories
8.3g - Fat
70.9g - Carbs
11.8g - Protein
9.2g - Sugars

Ingredients

- 2 medium-sized tomatoes, diced
- 2 cups water
- 1/2 teaspoon white pepper, or more to your liking
- 1 teaspoon salt
- 1 cup red bell pepper, thinly sliced
- 2 Serrano peppers, thinly sliced
- 2 cucumbers, cored and diced
- 2 red onions, chopped
- 1 ½ cups brown rice
- 3/4 cup crumbled Feta cheese

Directions

1. Choose the "RICE/RISOTTO" function. Add the rice and water to the Power Pressure Cooker XL. Close and lock the lid. Set the cooking time to 18 minutes.
2. Open the cooker using a Natural pressure release. Allow the rice to cool completely.
3. Add the remaining ingredients. Give it a gentle stir; serve well-chilled. Bon appétit!

14. Pumpkin Quinoa Delight

You can chill the cooked quinoa and use this as a base for an easy and healthy salad. Please bear in mind that quinoa easily picks up flavors of the ingredients it's cooked with.

Servings 4

Ready in about 15 minutes

NUTRITIONAL INFORMATION (Per Serving)

185 - Calories
2.9g - Fat
33.9g - Carbs
6.9g - Protein
2.6g - Sugars

Ingredients

- 1 ¼ cups canned pumpkin puree
- 1/2 teaspoon ground cloves
- 1/2 teaspoon freshly grated nutmeg
- 1/4 teaspoon salt
- 1/3 teaspoon ground cinnamon
- 1 ½ cups water
- 1 cup uncooked quinoa, well rinsed

Directions

1. Choose the "FISH/VEGETABLES/STEAM" function. Add all the components to the Power Pressure Cooker XL. Next, lock the lid and switch the pressure release valve to closed.
2. Set the cooking time to 2 minutes. Let the quinoa stand for 10 minutes.
3. Now, use a Quick pressure release and remove the lid according to the manufacturer's directions.
4. Taste and adjust the seasonings. Serve at once and enjoy!

15. Mediterranean Tomato-Basil Soup

Ripe tomatoes, potatoes, and aromatic herbs are all cooked together in this hearty soup for an appetizing lunch. You can substitute basil leaves for fresh chopped chives. Enjoy!

Servings 6

Ready in about 30 minutes

NUTRITIONAL INFORMATION (Per Serving)

130 - Calories
3.0g - Fat
24.2g - Carbs
4.0g - Protein
8.5g - Sugars

Ingredients

- 3 garlic cloves, peeled and finely minced
- 2 potatoes, peeled and chopped
- 1 cup onions, chopped
- 1 teaspoon dried oregano
- 1/2 teaspoon salt
- 1/2 teaspoon ground cumin
- 1 teaspoon celery seeds
- 1/2 teaspoon grated nutmeg
- 1 teaspoon fennel seeds
- 3 pounds tomatoes, chopped
- 1/2 cup packed fresh basil leaves
- 1 cup cream

Directions

1. Choose the "SOUP/STEW" function. Place the tomatoes, onions, potatoes, garlic, dried oregano, and salt into the Power Pressure Cooker XL; now, add the cumin, celery seeds, nutmeg, and fennel seeds.
2. After that, pour in 2 cups of water. Lock the lid onto the pot.
3. Set the cooking time to 22 minutes. Reduce the pressure naturally.
4. Carefully open the Power Pressure Cooker XL. Afterwards, stir in the cream and basil leaves. Serve at once and enjoy!

16. Autumn Harvest Soup

Never underestimate the importance of a good healthy soup at lunchtime. Be inspired by root vegetables and amaze your family!

Servings 6

Ready in about 45 minutes

NUTRITIONAL INFORMATION (Per Serving)

145 - Calories
8.7g - Fat
12.8g - Carbs
4.7g - Protein
3.3g - Sugars

Ingredients

- 4 cups chicken broth
- 3 ½ cups water
- 1 cup celery stalks, chopped
- 1 cup parsnips, chopped
- 1 cup shallots, finely chopped
- 2 Serrano peppers, seeded and chopped
- 1 ½ cups carrots, chopped
- 1/2 teaspoon ground cumin
- 1/2 teaspoon fennel seeds
- 1 teaspoon granulated garlic
- 1/2 stick butter, softened

Directions

1. Choose the "SOUP/STEW" function and melt the butter for a minute or so. Then, stir in the Serrano peppers, shallots, parsnip, carrots, and celery; sauté the ingredients for 6 minutes.
2. Stir in the rest of the above ingredients. Now, lock the lid and switch the pressure release valve to closed; set the timer for 35 minutes.
3. Once the cooking is complete, the Power Pressure Cooker XL will automatically switch to "KEEP WARM/CANCEL". When the steam is completely released, remove the cooker's lid.
4. Serve hot and enjoy.

17. Classic Italian Caponata

Caponata is a traditional Sicilian eggplant (aubergine) dish
that is cooked perfectly in the Power Pressure Cooker XL.
Serve with olives at room temperature.

Servings 4

Ready in about
40 minutes

**NUTRITIONAL
INFORMATION**
(Per Serving)

171 - Calories
16.9g - Fat
6.0g - Carbs
0.9g - Protein
2.5g - Sugars

Ingredients

- 1 cup red onion, sliced
- 2 tablespoons red wine vinegar
- 1/3 cup olive oil
- 2 cups eggplant, unpeeled and cubed
- 1 tablespoon salt
- 3 garlic cloves, chopped
- 1/2 cup fresh basil, chopped

Directions

1. Firstly, generously sprinkle the eggplant cubes with salt; let them stand in a colander at least 30 minutes. Rinse the eggplant in water; squeeze them and reserve.
2. Choose the "FISH/VEGETABLES/STEAM" function; heat the oil and sauté the eggplant, garlic, and red onion until they are tender.
3. Stir in the red wine. Cover with the lid and set the cooking time to 7 minutes. Switch the pressure release valve to open. When the steam is completely released, remove the cooker's lid.
4. Serve sprinkled with fresh basil leaves and olives if desired. Bon appétit!

18. Creamy Potato Soup

A thick and creamy vegetarian soup to get you through busy days. The recipe is very easy to make and yields even 6 servings. Serve with homemade cornbread if desired.

Servings 6

Ready in about 45 minutes

NUTRITIONAL INFORMATION
(Per Serving)

195 - Calories
4.3g - Fat
30.5g - Carbs
9.0g - Protein
4.9g - Sugars

Ingredients

- 4 cups vegetable broth
- 1 ½ cups carrots, sliced
- 1 cup celery, chopped
- 1 cup celery stalk, thinly sliced
- 1 cup yellow onion, chopped
- 1 teaspoon red pepper flakes, crushed
- 1 ½ tablespoons ground chia seeds
- 1/2 teaspoon ground black pepper, to taste
- 1 teaspoon salt
- 2 tablespoons fresh basil leaves, finely chopped
- 2 pounds potatoes, peeled and diced
- 1 cup spinach leaves, chopped
- 1/2 cup sharp Cheddar cheese, grated

Directions

1. Press the "SOUP/STEW" key. Simply throw all the ingredients, except for the cheese, into the Power Pressure Cooker XL.
2. Place the lid on the Power Pressure Cooker XL, lock the lid and switch the pressure release valve to closed. Now, adjust the timer to 40 minutes.
3. When the steam is completely released, remove the cooker's lid.
4. Lastly, puree the soup with an immersion blender. Ladle the soup into six bowls; top with the grated Cheddar cheese.

19. Garden Vegetable Soup

Feed a crowd with this hearty and healthy soup that is made of vitamin-packed veggies. Serve with hot, crusty rolls.

Servings 8

Ready in about 20 minutes

NUTRITIONAL INFORMATION (Per Serving)

120 - Calories
6.0g - Fat
13.0g - Carbs
5.5g - Protein
3.8g - Sugars

Ingredients

- 2 cups canned diced tomatoes
- 1 cup fennel bulb, trimmed and chopped
- 3/4 pound green beans, trimmed and cut into 1-inch pieces
- 5 cups vegetable broth
- 2 tablespoons butter
- 1 tablespoon olive oil
- 1/2 teaspoon ground black pepper
- 1/2 teaspoon salt
- 1/2 teaspoon dill weed
- 1 cup onions, cut into rings
- 1 ½ cups fresh corn kernels

Directions

1. Press the "SOUP/STEW" key and melt the oil and butter. Sauté the onion, stirring often, until softened, about 4 minutes. Stir in the vegetable broth, tomatoes, fennel bulb, dill, salt, and the black pepper.
2. Place the lid on the Power Pressure Cooker XL, lock the lid and switch the pressure release valve to closed. Cook for 10 minutes.
3. Use a quick release and open the cooker. Stir in the corn kernels and green beans.
4. Lock the lid back onto your Power Pressure Cooker XL. Continue cooking for 5 minutes longer. Use a quick release and carefully remove the lid. Serve in individual bowls.

20. Wheat Berry with Veggies and Greek Yogurt

Greek yogurt is much creamier than regular yogurt; it has less sugar and more carbs. Greek yogurt is packed with proteins, calcium, probiotics, vitamin B12, and potassium.

Servings 4

Ready in about 30 minutes

NUTRITIONAL INFORMATION (Per Serving)

150 - Calories
11.9g - Fat
8.3g - Carbs
2.6g - Protein
5.1g - Sugars

Ingredients

- 1 cup sweet onions, peeled and sliced
- 1 cup celery stalks, chopped
- 1/2 stick butter
- 1/4 teaspoon black pepper, or more to taste
- 1 teaspoon salt
- 1 cup carrots, thinly sliced
- 1 ½ cups white wheat berries, soaked overnight in lots of water
- 1/2 cup Greek yogurt, for garnish

Directions

1. Choose the "RICE/RISOTTO" function. In your Power Pressure Cooker XL, combine the white wheat berries with 6 cups water.
2. In a pan, melt the butter over medium heat. Then, sauté the sweet onions until tender and translucent. Add the salt and ground black pepper.
3. Place the lid on the Power Pressure Cooker XL. Cook the wheat berries together with the carrots and celery until they are tender, about 25 minutes. Switch the pressure release valve to open.
4. When the steam is released completely, remove the lid. Now, add the sautéed sweet onions and stir well.
5. Serve topped with Greek yogurt.

POULTRY

21. Chicken Liver Pâté Spread

Make this pâté a day ahead to allow the flavors to develop.
Serve with wheat crackers or warm toast.

Servings 16

**Ready in about
15 minutes**

**NUTRITIONAL
INFORMATION**
(Per Serving)

80 - Calories
3.9g - Fat
1.2g - Carbs
7.0g - Protein
0.0g - Sugars

Ingredients

- 2 tablespoons butter
- 2 teaspoons olive oil
- 1 teaspoon dried basil
- 1 tablespoon dried sage
- 2 sprigs dried thyme
- 1/2 teaspoon ground black pepper, to taste
- 1 teaspoon salt
- 1 pound chicken livers
- 3 anchovies in oil
- 1 cup leek, roughly chopped
- 1/3 cup rum

Directions

1. Press the "CHICKEN/MEAT" key. Put the olive oil into the Power Pressure Cooker XL; sauté the leeks. Then, add the chicken livers and cook until the livers are seared.
2. Pour in the rum. Close and lock the lid of your Power Pressure Cooker XL. Set the cooking time to 10 minutes.
3. Switch the pressure release valve to open. When the steam is released completely, remove the lid.
4. Add the remaining ingredients and stir to combine. Serve well chilled with your favorite rustic bread.

22. Chicken and Kale Stew

This hearty stew features tender ground chicken simmered with tomatoes, root vegetables and kale. Crisp white wine adds just the right amount of tanginess to this robust stew.

Servings 8

Ready in about 20 minutes

NUTRITIONAL INFORMATION (Per Serving)

235 - Calories
8.0g - Fat
14.9g - Carbs
23.1g - Protein
2.8g - Sugars

Ingredients

- 1 cup tomatoes, seeded and chopped
- 1 pound ground chicken
- 1/4 teaspoon ground black pepper
- 1/2 teaspoon salt
- 2 sprigs dried thyme
- 1 teaspoon red pepper flakes, crushed
- 1 teaspoon marjoram
- 3 teaspoons olive oil
- 1/2 cup celery stalk, chopped
- 1 cup carrots, diced
- 1 cup onions, diced
- 1/3 cup white wine
- 1 cup kale leaves, chopped
- 7 cups chicken broth
- 10 ounces noodles, cooked

Directions

1. Press the "SOUP/STEW" key and melt the olive oil. Once hot, add the ground chicken and all seasonings. Cook until the chicken has browned.
2. Add the onion, carrot, and celery; cook for about 6 minutes. Pour in the wine to deglaze the pot.
3. Add the remaining ingredients, minus the cooked noodles. Stir to combine and place the lid on your Power Pressure Cooker XL and lock. Switch the pressure release valve to closed.
4. Set the cooking time to 10 minutes. Once the timer reaches 0, the Power Pressure Cooker XL will automatically switch to "KEEP WARM/CANCEL".
5. Switch the pressure release valve to open. When the steam is released completely, remove the lid.
6. Serve warm with cooked noodles.

23. Chicken, Artichoke and Rice Casserole

Treat your family to a comforting bowl of something fabulous like this rich and hearty casserole. The casserole is a family-friendly recipe that cooks perfectly in the Power Pressure Cooker XL!

Servings 6

Ready in about 25 minutes

NUTRITIONAL INFORMATION (Per Serving)

595 - Calories
30.3g - Fat
49.8g - Carbs
30.9g - Protein
4.9g - Sugars

Ingredients

- 1 teaspoon minced garlic
- 1 cup onions, chopped
- 1/3 cup rosé wine
- 1 pound hot Italian sausage, cut into pieces
- 4 boneless, skinless chicken thighs
- 3 tablespoons olive oil
- 1 ½ cups chicken stock
- 11 ounces artichoke hearts, quartered
- 1 teaspoon paprika
- 1/2 teaspoon ground black pepper
- 1 teaspoon salt
- 2 Serrano peppers, stemmed, cored, and chopped
- 26 ounces canned whole tomatoes, roughly chopped
- 1 ½ cups long-grain white rice

Directions

1. Press the "RICE/RISOTTO" key. Heat the olive oil and brown the sausage, turning periodically, for about 5 minutes. Transfer to a large-sized bowl.
2. Add the chicken and brown, turning occasionally, for approximately 5 minutes. Transfer to the bowl with the sausage.
3. Stir in the onion and Serrano peppers. Cook, while stirring frequently, until the onion is translucent, or about 3 minutes. Add the garlic and cook until aromatic.
4. Pour in the wine; bring to a simmer. Continue simmering until the wine has reduced to a thick glaze. Stir in the tomatoes, stock, white rice, artichoke hearts, paprika, salt, and ground black pepper.
5. Return the reserved sausage and the chicken to the cooker. Give it a good stir. Lock the lid onto the Power Pressure Cooker XL. Cook for 10 minutes.
6. Use a Quick release function and open your Power Pressure Cooker XL. Stir once again before serving.

124. Chicken Curry Soup

If you love curry, the Power Pressure Cooker XL is a great tool to prepare this all-in-one meal while saving you time and money. You can add chopped smoked bacon to enrich the flavor.

Servings 4

Ready in about 25 minutes

NUTRITIONAL INFORMATION (Per Serving)

320 - Calories
23.4g - Fat
19.4g - Carbs
11.5g - Protein
8.9g - Sugars

Ingredients

- 1 pound chicken breast, chopped
- 2 ½ cups water
- 8 ounces frozen okra
- 1/2 teaspoon ground ginger
- 1/2 teaspoon curry powder
- 8 ounces sugar snap peas
- 1 ½ cups coconut milk
- 8 ounces frozen carrots

Directions

1. Choose the "SOUP/STEW" function. Put all the ingredients into your Power Pressure Cooker XL.
2. Place the lid on the Power Pressure Cooker XL and lock. Cook for 20 minutes.
3. Once the timer reaches 0, the Power Pressure Cooker XL will automatically switch to "KEEP WARM". Press the "CANCEL" key. Switch the pressure release valve to open.
4. When the steam is released completely, remove the lid. Serve hot and enjoy!

25. Country Chicken and Vegetable Soup

We all know that soup is the very important meal, but many of us don't have the time to make healthy and satisfying soup. Don't settle for store-bought instant soup and make this easy, homey soup just like your grandma used to make.

Servings 6

Ready in about 40 minutes

NUTRITIONAL
INFORMATION
(Per Serving)

167 - Calories
2.8g - Fat
11.1g - Carbs
23.5g - Protein
3.1g - Sugars

Ingredients

- 1/2 pound potatoes, diced
- 4 ½ cups chicken stock
- 1 ½ cups carrots, trimmed and chopped
- 1 cup onion, peeled and diced
- 1/2 teaspoon freshly cracked black pepper, to taste
- 1 teaspoon salt
- 4 frozen chicken breast halves, boneless and skinless

Directions

1. Choose the "CHICKEN/MEAT" function. Simply put all of the above ingredients into your Power Pressure Cooker XL.
2. Close and lock the lid. Set the cooking time to 30 minutes. Then switch the pressure release valve to open.
3. When the steam is completely released, remove the lid. Serve right away!

26. Delicious Spring Chili

Here's an easy recipe for chicken chili that will nourish your appetite and delight your taste buds! The recipe calls for spring plants but you can make this chili all year long by using winter onions instead of green onions.

Servings 8

Ready in about 35 minutes

NUTRITIONAL INFORMATION (Per Serving)

317 - Calories
4.1g - Fat
29.1g - Carbs
39.6g - Protein
2.1g - Sugars

Ingredients

- 1 ¾ pounds coarse ground chicken
- 2 cups water
- 1 tablespoon green garlic, minced
- 1 teaspoon cumin powder
- 1 large-sized green chili, diced
- 1 teaspoon celery seeds
- 1 ½ cups green onions, chopped
- 1 ¾ cups dry pinto beans
- 16 ounces canned beef broth
- 1 cup tomato, diced

Directions

1. Press the "BEANS/LENTILS" key and the brown ground chicken for 5 minutes; deglaze a pan with beef broth.
2. Add the rest of the above ingredients. Place the lid on the Power Pressure Cooker XL and lock the lid; switch the pressure release valve to closed.
3. Cook for 25 minutes. Remove the lid according to the manufacturer's instructions.
4. Serve right away, topped with fresh chives, if desired.

27. Chicken and Navy Bean Soup

———————— ∼ ————————

Hearty and filling, a hot bowl of bean soup is sure to warm your body and soul, no matter what the season. Navy beans is a staple food you should always have on hand.

Servings 6

———

Ready in about
35 minutes

———

**NUTRITIONAL
INFORMATION**
(Per Serving)

459 - Calories
13.0g - Fat
62.4g - Carbs
26.4g - Protein
6.0g - Sugars

Ingredients

- 3/4 pound cooked chicken breast, chopped
- 2 cups chicken stock
- 16 ounces canned stewed tomatoes
- 1/2 teaspoon cayenne pepper
- 1/2 teaspoon salt
- 1/4 teaspoon ground black pepper, chopped
- 20 ounces canned navy beans, rinsed and drained
- 3 teaspoons olive oil
- 1 cup sour cream
- 1/2 cup fresh cilantro, chopped

Directions

1. Choose the "SOUP/STEW" function. Place all the ingredients, except for the cilantro, in the inner pot of the Power Pressure Cooker XL.
2. Next, lock the lid; press the time adjustment button until you reach 30 minutes.
3. Serve warm garnished with fresh cilantro.

28. Rigatoni with Chicken and Parmesan

It's easy to make the most sophisticated pasta recipes! Just gather the ingredients, throw them all into the Power Pressure Cooker XL, and let them cook while you relax.

Servings 4

Ready in about 20 minutes

NUTRITIONAL INFORMATION (Per Serving)

643 - Calories
14.2g - Fat
68.8g - Carbs
57.4g - Protein
2.9g - Sugars

Ingredients

- 1 ¾ cups tomato paste
- 1/2 teaspoon salt
- 1/2 tablespoon fresh sage
- 1 teaspoon dried thyme
- 1/2 tablespoon fresh basil, chopped
- 1/4 teaspoon ground black pepper, or more to taste
- 1 ½ pounds chicken, chopped
- 1 heaping teaspoon minced garlic
- 1 cup leeks, chopped
- 1 package dry rigatoni pasta
- 2 tablespoons peanut oil
- 1/2 cup Parmesan cheese, grated

Directions

1. Press the "CHICKEN/MEAT" key and warm the peanut oil. Cook the chicken, leeks, and garlic till they're thoroughly cooked, approximately 6 minutes. Press the "CANCEL" button.
2. Add the rest of the above ingredients, except for the Parmesan cheese. Now, choose the "BEANS/ LENTILS" function. Close and lock the lid. Cook for 4 minutes.
3. Next, release the pressure by using a Quick pressure release. When the steam is completely released, remove the lid. Serve topped with grated Parmesan cheese.

29. Chicken with Pears and Sweet Onion

Get ready for this unusual sweet and savory chicken to kick things up! If you're not a fan of fruit and meat combo, just substitute the pears for sweet potatoes.

Servings 6

Ready in about 25 minutes

NUTRITIONAL INFORMATION (Per Serving)

292 - Calories
6.7g - Fat
11.6g - Carbs
44.4g - Protein
7.1g - Sugars

Ingredients

- 1 cup chicken stock
- 3 teaspoons butter
- 3 small-sized firm pears, peeled, cored, and sliced
- 1/2 cup sweet onions, chopped
- 1/2 teaspoon ground black pepper
- 1 teaspoon cayenne pepper
- 1 teaspoon salt
- 10 boneless, skinless chicken thighs, trimmed
- 2 tablespoons balsamic vinegar
- 1 teaspoon dried dill weed

Directions

1. Press the "CHICKEN/MEAT" key and melt the butter. Sprinkle the chicken with the salt, cayenne pepper, and black pepper; brown it lightly on both sides, turning once or twice. Set it aside.
2. Add the remaining ingredients. Add the browned chicken into the mixture.
3. Place the lid on the Power Pressure Cooker XL. Cook about 20 minutes or until the chicken is tender.
4. When the steam is completely released, unlock and open the Power Pressure Cooker XL. Stir well and serve.

30. Jalapeño Chicken Thighs

Here is one of the most delicious recipes for spicy chicken thighs! If you're not a fan of spicy wings, adjust the number of jalapeños to your liking. Pair these wings with steamed rice or mashed potatoes.

Servings 6

Ready in about 30 minutes

NUTRITIONAL INFORMATION (Per Serving)

262 - Calories
7.1g - Fat
2.4g - Carbs
44.5g - Protein
1.1g - Sugars

Ingredients

- 1/2 teaspoon ground black pepper
- 1 teaspoon ground cumin
- 1 teaspoon salt
- 1/2 teaspoon dried thyme
- 1/3 cup chicken broth
- 1 cup spring onions, green and white parts, thinly sliced
- 10 boneless, skinless chicken thighs, trimmed
- 1 teaspoon minced garlic
- 1 teaspoon packed dark brown sugar
- 2 fresh jalapeño chilies, stemmed, seeded, and minced
- 1 ½ tablespoons balsamic vinegar
- 1 tablespoon olive oil

Directions

1. Press the "CHICKEN/MEAT" key and heat the oil. Mix the chicken, thyme, cumin, salt, and black pepper. Set aside.
2. Cook the jalapeño pepper, spring onions, and garlic; stir often until they become soft, approximately 3 minutes.
3. Add the chicken mixture, scraping every speck of spice, to the Power Pressure Cooker XL; cook about 5 minutes, stirring occasionally, until lightly browned. Pour in the broth and vinegar; stir in the brown sugar until dissolved.
4. Place the lid on the Power Pressure Cooker XL, lock the lid and switch the pressure release valve to closed.
5. Cook for a further 17 minutes. Use a Quick release method, unlock, and open the Power Pressure Cooker XL. Stir well and serve immediately. Bon appétit!

31. Classic Chicken Curry

Coconut milk gives a wonderful texture to this classic chicken meal. It contains lauric acid, which has been shown to promote bone health.

Servings 6

Ready in about 20 minutes

NUTRITIONAL INFORMATION (Per Serving)

491 - Calories
30.4g - Fat
8.7g - Carbs
45.9g - Protein
3.5g - Sugars

Ingredients

- 2 tablespoons canola oil
- 1 cup carrots, chopped
- 1 ½ cups coconut milk
- 2 teaspoons ginger, freshly grated
- 1/2 teaspoon celery seeds
- 1/2 teaspoon ground black pepper
- 1 teaspoon salt
- 1/2 teaspoon ground cumin
- 1/2 teaspoon fennel seeds
- 1 teaspoon ground turmeric
- 1 teaspoon minced garlic
- 2 pounds chicken breasts, cut into bite-size chunks
- 1 cup leeks, chopped
- 1/2 cup fresh parsley leaves, roughly chopped

Directions

1. Press the "CHICKEN/MEAT" key. Now, heat the oil; sauté the leeks, garlic, carrot and ginger in hot oil; cook until they're just tender.
2. Add the fennel seeds, celery seeds, cumin, and turmeric, and cook for an additional 3 minutes.
3. Stir in the remaining ingredients, except for the parsley.
4. Place the lid on the Power Pressure Cooker XL, lock the lid and switch the pressure release valve to closed; cook for 10 minutes.
5. Use a Quick release method, unlock, and open the Power Pressure Cooker XL. Serve warm garnished with fresh parsley leaves.

32. Party Hot Chicken Wings

Rich and spicy, this chicken wings call for a combination of hot sauce and butter; feel free to use whatever hot sauce you have on hand.

Servings 8

Ready in about 20 minutes

NUTRITIONAL INFORMATION
(Per Serving)

371 - Calories
9.9g - Fat
0.6g - Carbs
65.9g - Protein
0.0g - Sugars

Ingredients

- 16 chicken wings, frozen
- 1 sprig thyme
- 1 cup hot sauce
- 1/2 teaspoon salt
- 1/2 teaspoon freshly ground black pepper
- 2 tablespoons butter, melted

Directions

1. Choose the "CHICKEN/MEAT" function. Add the melted butter and hot sauce to the Power Pressure Cooker XL; mix to combine well.
2. Add the remaining ingredients. Place the lid on the Power Pressure Cooker XL, lock the lid and switch the pressure release valve to closed.
3. Cook for 15 minutes. Press the "CANCEL" key. Switch the pressure release valve to open. When the steam is completely released, remove the lid.
4. Serve warm with a dipping sauce of choice.

33. Saucy Turkey Wings

Lots of cranberries and orange juice, plus spices to balance out the sweetness of the fruit, make this recipe a winner for your family lunch!

Servings 4

Ready in about 40 minutes

NUTRITIONAL INFORMATION (Per Serving)

463 - Calories
29.0g - Fat
13.0g - Carbs
34.6g - Protein
6.4g - Sugars

Ingredients
- 1 pound turkey wings
- 1 stick butter, at room temperature
- 2 cups vegetable stock
- 2 cups cranberries
- 1/3 cup orange juice
- 2 onions, sliced into rings
- 1/2 teaspoon ground black pepper, to your liking
- 1/2 teaspoon cayenne pepper
- 1 teaspoon salt

Directions
1. Choose the "CHICKEN/MEAT" function and melt the butter. Brown the turkey wings on all sides. Season with the salt, black pepper, and cayenne pepper.
2. Now, add the onion rings and cranberries. Pour in the orange juice and the vegetable stock. Place the lid on the Power Pressure Cooker XL, lock the lid and switch the pressure release valve to closed. Cook for 25 minutes.
3. Press the "CANCEL" key. Switch the pressure release valve to open. When the steam is completely released, remove the lid.
4. Afterwards, preheat a broiler. Cook the wings under the broiler for about 7 minutes.
5. While the wings are broiling, press the "CHICKEN/MEAT" key again and cook the sauce uncovered in order to reduce the liquid content. Spoon the sauce over the wings and serve.

34. Honey Chicken Wings

Honey adds a little bit of sweetness to balance the spices in this recipe. If you like mild-tasting wings you can cut the shallot powder down to 1/2 teaspoon.

Servings 5

Ready in about 35 minutes

NUTRITIONAL INFORMATION (Per Serving)

346 - Calories
5.5g - Fat
19.0g - Carbs
52.7g - Protein
18.6g - Sugars

Ingredients

- 1/3 cup honey
- 1/2 teaspoon garlic powder
- 1 teaspoon coriander
- 1/2 teaspoon cumin powder
- 2 tablespoons apple cider vinegar
- 12 chicken wings
- 1 tablespoon shallot powder
- 1/4 teaspoon ground black pepper
- 1 teaspoon salt

Directions

1. Choose the "CHICKEN/MEAT" function. Place the chicken wings in your Power Pressure Cooker XL.
2. Place the lid on the Power Pressure Cooker XL, lock the lid and switch the pressure release valve to closed. Cook for 15 minutes. Reserve the liquid.
3. Preheat your oven to 390 degrees F.
4. Transfer the chicken wings to the oven and roast them until the skin is crispy. Remove the chicken from the oven and set aside in a baking dish, keeping them warm.
5. Add the rest of the above ingredients to the Power Pressure Cooker XL with the chicken broth; choose the "CHICKEN/MEAT" function.
6. Cook for 12 minutes, stirring continuously. Pour the sauce over the chicken wings, and serve.

35. Fried Rice with Chicken

This is a classic and belly-warming dish that everyone will love. It is also kid-friendly and can be served as a festive dinner and family lunch.

Servings 6

Ready in about 25 minutes

NUTRITIONAL INFORMATION
(Per Serving)

431 - Calories
9.6g - Fat
64.5g - Carbs
19.5g - Protein
1.3g - Sugars

Ingredients

- 1/2 stick butter, softened
- 3 ½ cups water
- 2 cups chicken, cut into chunks
- 2 medium-sized carrots, thinly sliced
- 2 ½ cups multi-grain rice
- 2 tablespoons apple cider vinegar
- 1/2 teaspoon ground black pepper, to taste
- 1 teaspoon salt
- 1 teaspoon dried basil
- 1 teaspoon dried dill weed
- 1/2 cup green onions, chopped

Directions

1. Choose the "RICE/RISOTTO" function. Add all of the above ingredients to your Power Pressure Cooker XL.
2. Place the lid on the Power Pressure Cooker XL, lock the lid and switch the pressure release valve to closed. Set the timer for 20 minutes.
3. Once the cooking is complete, press the "CANCEL" key.
4. When the steam has been released, remove the lid. Serve right now.

36. Chicken and Green Pea Soup

Canned tomatoes, chicken and green peas are natural allies in this healthy and hearty soup. Serve with a generous spoonful of Greek yogurt or mashed cauliflower swirled into each serving.

Servings 6

Ready in about 30 minutes

NUTRITIONAL
INFORMATION
(Per Serving)

227 - Calories
3.3g - Fat
21.2g - Carbs
28.4g - Protein
9.8g - Sugars

Ingredients

- 1 cup onions, chopped
- 1 teaspoon minced garlic
- 20 ounces canned diced tomatoes
- 2 chicken breasts, boneless, skinless and diced
- 1/4 teaspoon ground black pepper
- 1/2 teaspoon salt
- 1 teaspoon dried dill weed
- 1 teaspoon dried marjoram
- 4 cups vegetable stock
- 1 cup carrots, diced
- 1 cup celery rib, chopped
- 1/2 cup celery stalk, chopped
- 18 ounces green peas

Directions

1. Choose the "SOUP/STEW" function. Add all of the above ingredients, except for the peas, to your Power Pressure Cooker XL. Lock the lid and switch the pressure release valve to closed.
2. Cook for 20 minutes; use a Quick release method to drop the pressure.
3. Unlock and open the Power Pressure Cooker XL. Stir in the green peas. Then, seal the lid and wait for 7 minutes to warm up and blanch the peas. Serve hot with cornbread.

37. Ground Turkey Bean Chili

Make room for a 5-star meal! No hot sauce here. Just purely rich beans, meat and creamy goodness.

Servings 8

Ready in about
20 minutes

NUTRITIONAL
INFORMATION
(Per Serving)

337 - Calories
18.6g - Fat
13.3g - Carbs
35.9g - Protein
2.4g - Sugars

Ingredients

- 2 cups water
- 2 ½ cups chicken stock
- 1/2 teaspoon celery seeds
- 1 cup onions, chopped
- 1 teaspoon chili powder
- 30 ounces canned beans, drained and rinsed well
- 2 tablespoons olive oil
- 2 pounds ground turkey
- 30 ounces canned diced tomatoes with green chilies
- 1/2 teaspoon cumin powder
- 1/2 cup Monterey Jack cheese, shredded

Directions

1. Press the "RICE/RISOTTO" key and melt the oil in your Power Pressure Cooker XL. Then, sauté the onions for 6 minutes. Add the ground turkey and cook until the meat has browned, 6 minutes more.
2. Stir in the remaining ingredients, except for the Monterey Jack cheese. Cover and cook for 6 minutes.
3. Switch the pressure release valve to open. When the steam is released, remove the cooker's lid.
4. Ladle into soup bowls and serve topped with the shredded Monterey Jack cheese. Bon appétit!

38. Chicken with Beans and Tomato

You can use any type of canned beans for this recipe, even though the recipe calls for red kidney beans. Also, if you can use homemade stewed tomatoes, it is absolutely worth the time invested.

Servings 6

Ready in about 20 minutes

NUTRITIONAL INFORMATION (Per Serving)

349 - Calories
7.6g - Fat
50.1g - Carbs
22.5g - Protein
5.2g - Sugars

Ingredients

- 1 pound chicken breast, chopped
- 3 teaspoons vegetable oil
- 16 ounces canned stewed tomatoes
- 1/4 teaspoon ground black pepper, chopped
- 1/2 teaspoon salt
- 1/2 teaspoon paprika
- 16 ounces canned red kidney beans, rinsed and drained
- 1/2 cup fresh parsley leaves, coarsely chopped
- 2 cups vegetable stock
- 1/3 cup sour cream

Directions

1. Choose the "SOUP/STEW" function.
2. Place the ingredients, except the parsley leaves, in the inner pot of the Power Pressure Cooker XL.
3. Next, place the lid on the Power Pressure Cooker XL; then, press the time adjustment button until you reach 15 minutes.
4. Press the "CANCEL" key. Switch the pressure release valve to open. When the steam is released completely, remove the cooker's lid.
5. Serve garnished with fresh parsley. Bon appétit!

39. Peppery Chicken Dip

When you are having friends over, the last thing you want to do is spend hours in the kitchen, preparing food. This dipping sauce is ready in less than 30 minutes and you can make it a day or two ahead and keep it in your refrigerator.

Servings 10

Ready in about 25 minutes

NUTRITIONAL INFORMATION (Per Serving)

136 - Calories
6.3g - Fat
5.7g - Carbs
14.0g - Protein
3.1g - Sugars

Ingredients

- 1 cup tomato puree, chopped
- 2 tablespoons canola oil
- 1 ½ teaspoons granulated garlic
- 3 teaspoons arrowroot
- 1 cup onion, finely chopped
- 1 pound ground chicken
- 1 ½ teaspoons dried basil
- 1/2 teaspoon ground black pepper to taste
- 1 teaspoon salt
- 1/2 teaspoon cayenne pepper
- 1 teaspoon dried thyme
- 2 Serrano peppers, seeded and chopped
- 2 bell peppers, seeded and chopped

Directions

1. Choose the "CHICKEN/MEAT" function and warm the canola oil. Cook the chicken in the hot oil for about 6 minutes, or until the meat is no longer pink.
2. Add the rest of the above ingredients. Next, place the lid on the Power Pressure Cooker XL; then, press the time adjustment button until you reach 15 minutes.
3. Press the "CANCEL" key. Switch the pressure release valve to open. When the steam is released completely, remove the cooker's lid. Serve warm or at room temperature.

40. Saucy Chicken Wings

Here's the recipe for the most delicious and the easiest chicken wings ever! While they're cooking, relax and enjoy a glass of wine as the entire house fills with the wonderful smells.

Servings 8

Ready in about 20 minutes

NUTRITIONAL INFORMATION (Per Serving)

285 - Calories
8.1g - Fat
0.5g - Carbs
49.5g - Protein
0.0g - Sugars

Ingredients

- 16 chicken wings, frozen
- 2 tablespoons butter
- 1 cup hot sauce

Directions

1. Choose the "SOUP/STEW" function. Add the butter and the hot sauce to the Power Pressure Cooker XL.
2. Throw in the wings. Place the lid on the Power Pressure Cooker XL, lock the lid and switch the pressure release valve to closed.
3. Cook for 15 minutes. Press the "CANCEL" key. Switch the pressure release valve to open. When the steam is completely released, remove the lid. Bon appétit!

PORK

41. Old-Fashioned Beans

Pinto beans are high in fiber and protein. This amazing food can reduce cholesterol levels, protect your heart and help lower risk of cancer.

Servings 8

Ready in about 30 minutes

NUTRITIONAL
INFORMATION
(Per Serving)

516 - Calories
19.4g - Fat
56.1g - Carbs
29.2g - Protein
3.0g - Sugars

Ingredients

- 1 ½ cups water
- 1 (1 1¼) package onion soup mix
- 1/4 cup olive oil
- 1/2 tablespoon brown sugar
- 1 tablespoon minced garlic
- 1 ½ pounds pinto beans, soaked overnight
- 2 teaspoons mustard
- 1/2 pound bacon slices, chopped
- 1 cup onions, chopped

Directions

1. Choose the "BEANS/LENTILS" function; warm the olive oil and cook the onions, garlic, and bacon for 6 minutes.
2. Add the soup mix and 1½ cup of water; cook for 6 more minutes. Now, add the beans and 4 cups of water.
3. Stir in the mustard and brown sugar. Place the lid on the Power Pressure Cooker XL, lock the lid and switch the pressure release valve to closed. Cook for an additional 15 minutes.
4. Press the "CANCEL" key. Switch the pressure release valve to open. When the steam is completely released, remove the lid. Serve immediately. Bon appétit!

42. Pork Ribs with Pearl Onions

—❀—

These are deliciously spicy and very addictive pork ribs. Feel free to adjust the amount of spices to your own personal taste.

Servings 4

Ready in about 35 minutes

NUTRITIONAL INFORMATION
(Per Serving)

361 - Calories
20.3g - Fat
11.9g - Carbs
32.0g - Protein
6.8g - Sugars

Ingredients

- 1 ½ cups tomato sauce
- 1 tablespoon minced garlic
- 1 ½ cups water
- 1/2 teaspoon ground black pepper
- 1 teaspoon salt
- 1/2 teaspoon dried marjoram
- 1 ¼ cups pearl onions
- 1 cup carrots, thinly sliced
- 1 pound pork ribs

Directions

1. Choose the "CHICKEN/MEAT" function.
2. Cook the ribs in the Power Pressure Cooker XL until browned. Pour in the water and the tomato sauce. Add the remaining ingredients.
3. Place the lid on the Power Pressure Cooker XL, lock the lid and switch the pressure release valve to closed. Press the "TIME ADJUSTMENT" key until you reach 30 minutes.
4. When the steam is completely released, remove the lid. Serve warm.

43. Tender Pork Butt with Mushrooms

This is a filling and comforting one-pot meal that is chock-full of nutritious vegetables and protein-packed meat. Making Sunday lunch for the whole family is easier than you think!

Servings 4

Ready in about 35 minutes

NUTRITIONAL INFORMATION (Per Serving)

254 - Calories
7.8g - Fat
3.9g - Carbs
37.0g - Protein
1.6g - Sugars

Ingredients

- 1/2 cup scallions, chopped
- 2 cups mushrooms, thinly sliced
- 1/4 teaspoon ground black pepper, to your liking
- 1 tablespoon coriander
- 1/2 teaspoon salt
- 1/3 cup dry red wine
- 1/2 cup chicken stock
- 1 teaspoon crushed garlic
- 1 pound pork butt, sliced
- 1/2 cup celery rib, chopped
- 1 cup celery stalk, chopped

Directions

1. Choose the "CHICKEN/MEAT" function.
2. Brown the pork in the Power Pressure Cooker XL for 10 minutes on all sides. Now, lay the sliced mushrooms over the ribs.
3. Pour in the wine and chicken stock. Throw in the remaining ingredients. Place the lid on the Power Pressure Cooker XL, lock the lid and switch the pressure release valve to closed. Press the "TIME ADJUSTMENT" key until you reach 20 minutes.
4. When the steam is completely released, remove the lid. Bon appétit!

44. Melt-in-Your-Mouth Pork Chops with Broccoli

An irresistible and affordable combination of tender pork chops and healthy vegetables that is perfect for cold winter nights when you need something tasty and satisfying.

Servings 4

Ready in about 30 minutes

NUTRITIONAL INFORMATION
(Per Serving)

302 - Calories
20.3g - Fat
5.1g - Carbs
20.8g - Protein
1.5g - Sugars

Ingredients

- 1/2 pound broccoli, chopped
- 2 medium-sized shallots, chopped
- 1 tablespoon coriander
- 1 ½ cups beef stock
- 1 teaspoon salt
- 1/2 teaspoon ground black pepper, or more to your liking
- 1 tablespoon peeled and crushed garlic
- 1 cup celery stalks, chopped
- 4 pork chops
- 1/3 cup sparkling wine

Directions

1. Press the "CHICKEN/MEAT" key.
2. Brown the pork chops for 10 minutes on all side. Throw in the remaining ingredients.
3. Place the lid on the Power Pressure Cooker XL, lock the lid and switch the pressure release valve to closed.
4. Press the "TIME ADJUSTMENT" key until you reach 15 minutes.
5. When the steam is completely released, remove the cooker's lid. Bon appétit!

45. Pork Tenderloin with Baby Carrots

This finger-licking pork tenderloin will delight your senses! Baby carrots are high in vitamin K, fiber, beta-carotene, potassium and antioxidants.

Servings 4

Ready in about 25 minutes

NUTRITIONAL INFORMATION (Per Serving)

265 - Calories
4.9g - Fat
17.4g - Carbs
33.2g - Protein
9.2g - Sugars

Ingredients

- 1 cup celery stalks, chopped
- 1 tablespoon peeled and crushed garlic
- 1/2 teaspoon red pepper, crushed
- 1/3 teaspoon fennel seeds
- 1/2 teaspoon cumin powder
- 1 pound baby carrots, thinly sliced
- 1 teaspoon salt
- 1/2 teaspoon ground black pepper, or more to your liking
- 1 pound pork tenderloin
- 1/3 cup dry red wine
- 2 white onions, chopped
- 1 ½ cups chicken broth

Directions

1. Press the "CHICKEN/MEAT" key. Brown the pork for 8 minutes on all side. Throw in the remaining ingredients.
2. Place the lid on the Power Pressure Cooker XL, lock the lid and switch the pressure release valve to closed.
3. Press the "TIME ADJUSTMENT" key until you reach 15 minutes.
4. When the steam is completely released, remove the cooker's lid.

46. Old-Fashioned Pork Belly

This recipe calls for sweet onions so that you can use Vidalia onions, Peruvian onions, sweet red onions, and so forth. Serve with warm pasta or rice.

Servings 6

Ready in about 40 minutes

NUTRITIONAL INFORMATION (Per Serving)

550 - Calories
30.6g - Fat
4.0g - Carbs
53.5g - Protein
1.4g - Sugars

Ingredients

- 5 medium-sized cloves garlic, sliced
- 1/2 teaspoon ground star anise
- 1 teaspoon grated fresh ginger
- 1 ½ pounds pork belly, sliced
- 2 ¼ cups water
- 1/4 cup cooking wine
- 1/2 cup sweet onions, peeled and chopped
- 1/3 cup soy sauce
- 1 teaspoon sugar

Directions

1. Press the "CHICKEN/MEAT" key and sear the pork belly on both sides, about 8 minutes. Add the remaining ingredients.
2. Place the lid on the Power Pressure Cooker XL, lock the lid and switch the pressure release valve to closed.
3. Press the "TIME ADJUSTMENT" key until you reach 25 minutes; cook until your meat is almost falling apart.
4. Once the timer reaches 0, the cooker will automatically switch to "KEEP WARM/CANCEL". Switch the pressure release valve to open.
5. When the steam is completely released, remove the cooker's lid. Serve right away!

47. Party Barbecue Pork

You can serve this saucy pork on a plate or make delicious barbecue sandwiches garnished with some pickles, mustard and tomato ketchup. It is good to freeze and pull out as needed.

Servings 16

Ready in about 55 minutes

NUTRITIONAL INFORMATION (Per Serving)

340 - Calories
7.1g - Fat
13.4g - Carbs
52.0g - Protein
9.5g - Sugars

Ingredients

- 1 ½ teaspoons garlic powder
- 1/2 teaspoon black pepper, or more to your liking
- 1 tablespoon onion powder
- 1 teaspoon sea salt
- 1/2 teaspoon cumin powder
- 7 pounds pork butt roast
- 20 ounces barbecue sauce

Directions

1. Press the "CHICKEN/MEAT" key.
2. Season the pork with the cumin powder, onion powder, garlic powder, salt and black pepper. Now, fill the cooker with enough water to cover.
3. Place the lid on the Power Pressure Cooker XL, lock the lid and switch the pressure release valve to closed.
4. Press the "TIME ADJUSTMENT" key until you reach 50 minutes. Switch the pressure release valve to open. When the steam is completely released, remove the cooker's lid.
5. Mix 2 cups of cooking juice with the barbecue sauce. Shred your pork and drizzle with the prepared sauce. Serve right now.

48. Pork Cutlets with Vegetables

There are so many ways to cook the pork cutlets, but the secret is to go nicely and slowly. Give this recipe a try and prepare the most appetizing cutlets with little effort.

Servings 4

Ready in about 35 minutes

NUTRITIONAL INFORMATION (Per Serving)

351 - Calories
4.4g - Fat
45.3g - Carbs
30.6g - Protein
28.6g - Sugars

Ingredients

- 4 pork cutlets
- 1 cup carrots, thinly sliced
- 1 cup parsnips, thinly sliced
- 1 cup onions, slice into rings
- 1 ½ cups BBQ sauce
- 1 ½ cups water

Directions

1. Press the "CHICKEN/MEAT" key. Place the pork cutlets in your Power Pressure Cooker XL. Pour in 1/2 cup of BBQ sauce and 1 ½ cups of water.
2. Add the onions, parsnips, and carrots. Lock the lid and switch the pressure release valve to closed.
3. Press the "TIME ADJUSTMENT" key until you reach 30 minutes. Switch the pressure release valve to open. When the steam is completely released, remove the cooker's lid.
4. Drizzle with the remaining 1 cup of BBQ sauce and serve right now.

49. Easy Braised Cabbage with Bacon

Here's a tangy, bright and comforting cabbage that you can plan even for busy weeknights. Top-notch chefs make braised cabbage with apples and a splash of balsamic vinegar. Lovely!

Servings 8

Ready in about 20 minutes

NUTRITIONAL
INFORMATION
(Per Serving)

103 - Calories
8.5g - Fat
4.4g - Carbs
2.9g - Protein
2.3g - Sugars

Ingredients

- 1 ½ cups beef broth
- 2 tablespoons lard
- 1/2 teaspoon ground black pepper
- 1 teaspoon salt
- 1 pound cabbage, shredded
- 4 slices bacon, cut into chunks

Directions

1. Press the "BEANS/LENTILS" key and cook the bacon for 6 minutes or until it's browned. Add the lard and stir until melted.
2. Add the cabbage to the Power Pressure Cooker XL; pour in the beef broth. Season with the salt and ground black pepper to taste. Stir to combine well.
3. Press the "CANCEL" key; then, press the "FISH/VEGETABLE/STEAM" key and increase the cook time to 10 minutes.
4. When the steam is completely released, remove the lid and press the "CANCEL" key. Serve warm.

50. Rigatoni with Sausage and Bacon

Everyone loves last minute meals that they can put together with ingredients from their pantry. In addition, if you use the Power Pressure Cooker XL, you will be able to make an amazing one-pot pasta recipe in 25 minutes!

Servings 4

Ready in about 25 minutes

NUTRITIONAL INFORMATION (Per Serving)

762 - Calories
43.0g - Fat
64.6g - Carbs
38.2g - Protein
3.3g - Sugars

Ingredients

- 1 (16-ounce) package dry rigatoni pasta
- 2 teaspoons olive oil
- 1 ¼ pounds sausage meat
- 2 ¼ cups tomato purée
- 1/2 teaspoon red pepper flakes crushed
- 1/2 teaspoon ground black pepper, or more to taste
- 1 teaspoon salt
- 4 slices bacon
- 1 cup leek, chopped
- 1/2 cup Parmigiano-Reggiano, grated
- 1 teaspoon fresh basil, chopped
- 1 teaspoon fresh sage
- 1 teaspoon minced garlic

Directions

1. Press the "BEANS/LENTILS" key and warm the olive oil. Cook the bacon for about 5 minutes. Now, add the sausage meat and cook for an additional 5 minutes, until it is browned and thoroughly cooked.
2. Add the leeks and garlic; sauté them for an additional 3 minutes. Now, add the tomato purée, salt, black pepper, and red pepper flakes. Add the rigatoni pasta; pour in the water to cover your pasta.
3. Press the "CANCEL" key; then, press the "SOUP/STEW" key and increase the cook time to 8 minutes. Lock the lid and switch the pressure release valve to closed.
4. When the steam is completely released, remove the lid. Throw in the sage, basil and the Parmigiano-Reggiano; stir until the cheese is completely melted. Enjoy!

51. Chili Bean Soup

If you're not a fan of spicy food, adjust the number of chili peppers to your liking. For a complete Mexican meal, serve these up with some tortilla chips or Spanish rice.

Servings 6

Ready in about 40 minutes

NUTRITIONAL INFORMATION
(Per Serving)

178 - Calories
4.2g - Fat
21.6g - Carbs
14.6g - Protein
8.4g - Sugars

Ingredients

- 1 ½ cups carrots, diced
- 16 ounces canned tomatoes, diced
- 1/2 pound ham bone
- 2 bay leaves
- 1 cup celery rib, diced
- 1 teaspoon kosher salt
- 1/2 teaspoon ground black pepper, or more to taste
- 1/2 teaspoon cumin powder
- 1/2 teaspoon garlic powder
- 1/2 teaspoon chili powder
- 1 chili pepper, minced
- 1 ½ cups dry beans, soaked in water overnight
- 1 cup red onion chopped

Directions

1. Press the "BEANS/LENTILS" key. Drain and rinse your beans.
2. Put the beans along with the ham bone and bay leaves into your Power Pressure Cooker XL; now, add just enough water to cover.
3. Lock the lid and switch the pressure release valve to closed. Press the "TIME ADJUSTMENT" key until you reach 10 minutes.
4. Discard the ham bone and bay leaves; now, add the other ingredients and stir to combine well.
5. Press the "SOUP/STEW" key; cook for 25 minutes. When the steam is completely released, remove the lid. Serve and enjoy!

52. Herbed Pasta with Bacon and Cheese

Get ready for rich and unusual pasta dish to kick things up!
A perfect mix of flavor and textures in this pasta dish will
amaze your family and friends

Servings 4

**Ready in about
20 minutes**

**NUTRITIONAL
INFORMATION
(Per Serving)**

652 - Calories
23.3g - Fat
98.5g - Carbs
17.4g - Protein
3.5g - Sugars

Ingredients

- 16 ounces dry pasta
- 1 cup yellow onions, finely chopped
- 1 teaspoon minced garlic
- 1 cup bacon
- 1/2 tablespoon fresh sage
- 1 sprig rosemary
- 1/2 tablespoon fresh basil, chopped
- 2 ½ cups tomato purée
- 1/2 teaspoon ground black pepper, or more to taste
- 1/2 teaspoon salt
- 1/2 teaspoon paprika
- 2 teaspoons lard, at room temperature
- 1/2 cup Cheddar cheese, grated

Directions

1. Press the "SOUP/STEW" key and warm the lard; cook the bacon for about 5 minutes. Add the onions and garlic; sauté until tender and fragrant, for 6 more minutes. Press the "CANCEL" key.
2. Now, add the tomato purée, paprika, salt, and black pepper.
3. Add the dry pasta and enough water to cover your pasta. Add rosemary, sage, and basil.
4. Choose the "BEANS/LENTILS" function. Lock the lid and switch the pressure release valve to closed.
5. Press the "TIME ADJUSTMENT" key until you reach 8 minutes. Once the timer reaches 0, the Power Pressure Cooker XL will automatically switch to "KEEP WARM/ CANCEL".
6. Switch the pressure release valve to open. When the steam is completely released, remove the lid. Add the Cheddar cheese and serve.

53. Traditional Pasta with Bolognese Sauce

Traditionally, we use spaghetti for this recipe; however, you can use any type of pasta noodles you like; orzo and farfalle even work well here.

Servings 6

Ready in about 20 minutes

NUTRITIONAL
INFORMATION
(Per Serving)

587 - Calories
36.9g - Fat
18.0g - Carbs
43.1g - Protein
5.3g - Sugars

Ingredients

- 2 teaspoons lard, at room temperature
- 20 ounces pasta noodles
- 1 ½ pounds tomato pasta sauce
- 1 teaspoon smashed garlic
- 1 teaspoon dried oregano
- 2 sprigs dried rosemary
- 1/2 teaspoon ground black pepper, to taste
- 1 teaspoon dried basil
- 1 teaspoon sea salt
- 1 pound ground pork
- 1/3 pound ground beef
- 1 cup onions, peeled and chopped

Directions

1. Press the "SOUP/STEW" key and warm the lard; sauté the onions, garlic, beef, and pork, stirring frequently, until they are tender, about 5 minutes. Press the "CANCEL" key.
2. Add the remaining ingredients. Choose the "BEANS/LENTILS". Lock the lid and switch the pressure release valve to closed. Press the "TIME ADJUSTMENT" key until you reach 10 minutes.
3. When the steam is completely released, remove the lid. Serve garnished with grated cheese if desired.

54. Christmas Spareribs with Pineapple

You can't go wrong with spareribs at Christmas. You could also try adding some diced chipotle or habanero peppers to give this dish an extra kick.

Servings 6

Ready in about 35 minutes

NUTRITIONAL
INFORMATION
(Per Serving)

678 - Calories
27.5g - Fat
44.8g - Carbs
60.6g - Protein
41.1g - Sugars

Ingredients

- 3 pounds spareribs, cut for serving
- 18 ounces canned pineapple
- 1/2 teaspoon black pepper, to taste
- 1/2 teaspoon coriander, ground
- 1 teaspoon salt
- 1 cup onions, sliced
- 1 (1-inch) piece ginger, finely chopped
- 1/2 teaspoon granulated garlic
- 1/2 cup tomato paste
- 3 teaspoons olive oil
- 1/3 cup tamari (soy) sauce
- 2 tablespoons apple cider vinegar
- Prepared cornstarch slurry

Directions

1. Press the "CHICKEN/MEAT" key and heat the olive oil; sauté the onions until tender, about 10 minutes.
2. Stir in the other ingredients, except for the cornstarch slurry. Lock the lid and switch the pressure release valve to closed.
3. Press the "TIME ADJUSTMENT" key until you reach 20 minutes.
4. Once the timer reaches 0, the Power Pressure Cooker XL will automatically switch to "KEEP WARM/ CANCEL". Switch the pressure release valve to open.
5. When the steam is completely released, remove the lid. Now, add the cornstarch slurry and stir until the sauce has thickened. Serve warm.

55. Rich Ham and Sausage Spaghetti

No matter the style, a great spaghetti recipe is not just about the recipe. It's also about the reliable kitchen tools. The Power Pressure Cooker XL spaghetti is one of the best pasta recipes you've ever tried!

Servings 6

Ready in about 20 minutes

NUTRITIONAL INFORMATION (Per Serving)

364 - Calories
8.2g - Fat
42.3g - Carbs
31.5g - Protein
9.1g - Sugars

Ingredients

- 24 ounces dried spaghetti
- 1 ¾ pounds pasta sauce
- 1/2 teaspoon spicy brown mustard
- 1 teaspoon crushed garlic
- 3 slices ham, chopped
- 2 teaspoons butter, softened
- 1/4 teaspoon ground black pepper, or more to taste
- 1 teaspoon dried basil
- 1/2 teaspoon sea salt
- 1/2 teaspoon dried oregano
- 1 cup onions, peeled and chopped
- 2 teaspoons grapeseed oil
- 1 pound pork sausage meat

Directions

1. Press the "CHICKEN/MEAT" key and melt the grape seed oil and butter.
2. Now, sauté the onions, garlic, sausage meat, and ham, stirring frequently, until they are tender, about 6 minutes. Press the "CANCEL" key. Add the remaining ingredients.
3. Choose the "BEANS/LENTILS" function. Lock the lid and switch the pressure release valve to closed. Press the "TIME ADJUSTMENT" key until you reach 10 minutes.
4. Once the timer reaches 0, the Power Pressure Cooker XL will automatically switch to "KEEP WARM/ CANCEL". Switch the pressure release valve to open.
5. When the steam is completely released, remove the lid. Serve at once.

56. Slow Cooker Meatloaf

There is no such thing as a saucy, slow cooker meatloaf! If you are missing grandma's classic meatloaf, here's the right recipe for you!

Servings 10

Ready in about 7 hours

NUTRITIONAL INFORMATION (Per Serving)

315 - Calories
18.7g - Fat
18.9g - Carbs
22.6g - Protein
7.7g - Sugars

Ingredients

For the Meatloaf:
- Non-stick cooking spray
- 1 ¼ cups milk
- 1 cup canned mushrooms, drained and chopped
- 1/2 teaspoon ground black pepper, or more to taste
- 1 teaspoon salt
- 1 cup onions, finely chopped
- 2 whole egg
- 2 sprigs dried thyme
- 1/2 teaspoon onion powder
- 3/4 teaspoon garlic powder
- 1 ½ cups rice, cooked
- 1 ½ pounds ground pork meat

For the Topping:
- 1 cup ketchup
- 1 teaspoon brown sugar

Directions

1. Press the "SLOW COOK" key. Lightly oil the inner pot of your Power Pressure Cooker XL with a non-stick cooking spray.
2. Mix all the ingredients for the meatloaf. Shape the mixture into a round loaf; transfer it to the Power Pressure Cooker XL.
3. Then, mix the ingredients for the topping. Place the topping over the meatloaf.
4. Lock the lid and switch the pressure release valve to closed. Press the "TIME ADJUSTMENT" key until you reach 7 hours.
5. Once the timer reaches 0, the Power Pressure Cooker XL will automatically switch to "KEEP WARM/ CANCEL". Switch the pressure release valve to open. When the steam is completely released, remove the lid. Enjoy!

57. Grandma's Juicy Pork Loin

Serve this mouth-watering pork loin as an elegant first course and treat your party guests! You can substitute rice wine vinegar for any white wine vinegar; champagne vinegar works well, too.

Servings 6

Ready in about 30 minutes

NUTRITIONAL INFORMATION (Per Serving)

613 - Calories
25.6g - Fat
43.2g - Carbs
50.8g - Protein
38.3g - Sugars

Ingredients

- 2 ½ pounds pork loin, cut for serving
- 16 ounces canned pineapple
- 1/2 teaspoon black pepper
- 1/2 teaspoon coriander, ground
- 1/2 teaspoon ginger, finely chopped
- 1/3 cup tamari sauce
- 1/4 cup rice wine vinegar
- 1/2 teaspoon granulated garlic
- 1 teaspoon salt
- 1 cup onions, sliced
- 1 tablespoon brown sugar
- 2 tablespoons olive oil
- 1/2 cup tomato paste
- 1 tablespoon cornstarch slurry

Directions

1. Choose the "SOUP/STEW" function and heat the oil; now, sauté the onions until just tender or about 6 minutes.
2. Stir in the rest of the above ingredients, except for the cornstarch slurry.
3. Lock the lid and switch the pressure release valve to closed. Cook for 20 minutes.
4. Once the timer reaches 0, the Power Pressure Cooker XL will automatically switch to "KEEP WARM/CANCEL". Switch the pressure release valve to open.
5. When the steam is completely released, remove the lid. Add the cornstarch slurry and stir until the juice has thickened. Serve warm and enjoy!

58. Maple Beans with Bacon

Loaded with rich and flavorful bacon, this deliciously satisfying beans are just as good as a family lunch, as it is served on weeknights. It's also great when reheated. Use any type of your favorite dry beans.

Servings 6

Ready in about 30 minutes

NUTRITIONAL INFORMATION (Per Serving)

307 - Calories
9.3g - Fat
36.8g - Carbs
20.2g - Protein
13.3g - Sugars

Ingredients

- 2 slices bacon, chopped
- 1/2 teaspoon ground black pepper, or more to taste
- 1 teaspoon sea salt
- 1 cup onions, diced
- 3 tablespoons tomato paste
- 2 ½ cups water
- 3 cups chicken stock
- 1 tablespoon maple syrup
- 3 ½ cups dry beans

Directions

1. Soak the beans overnight. Choose the "BEANS/ LENTILS" function.
2. Then, transfer the soaked beans to your Power Pressure Cooker XL.
3. Add the rest of the above ingredients. Place the lid on the Power Pressure Cooker XL, lock the lid and switch the pressure release valve to closed.
4. Press the "TIME ADJUSTMENT" key until you reach 25 minutes. Once the timer reaches 0, the Power Pressure Cooker XL will automatically switch to "KEEP WARM/CANCEL".
5. Switch the pressure release valve to open. When the steam is completely released, remove the lid. Bon appétit!

59. Holiday Ham with Pineapple

It's the holiday season! From now onwards, you can prepare traditional ham in no time and enjoy your holiday to the fullest.

Servings 8

Ready in about 1 hour

NUTRITIONAL INFORMATION (Per Serving)

324 - Calories
7.3g - Fat
44.4g - Carbs
21.2g - Protein
33.3g - Sugars

Ingredients

- 1 pound baby potatoes, and cubed
- 1 cup water
- 20 ounces canned crushed pineapple
- 2 tablespoons vegetable oil
- 2 pounds ham, cubed
- 5-6 freshly cracked black peppercorns
- 1 teaspoon salt
- 2 tablespoons brown sugar

Directions

1. Press the "CHICKEN/MEAT" key and heat the oil. Cook the ham cubes until lightly browned or about 6 minutes; add the water.
2. Next, stir in the potatoes, crushed pineapple, and brown sugar. Season with salt and black peppercorns.
3. Place the lid on the Power Pressure Cooker XL, lock the lid and switch the pressure release valve to closed. Cook for 50 minutes
4. When the Beep sounds, perform a Natural pressure release. When the steam is completely released, remove the lid. Bon appétit!

60. Root Vegetable and Pork Soup

A tasty and rich soup that has all the best flavors of the season, made with the healthiest ingredients in the world! Turnip can help you lower blood pressure and fight cancer. Parsnip prevents heart disease, obesity, diverticulitis and stroke.

Servings 6

Ready in about 40 minutes

NUTRITIONAL INFORMATION (Per Serving)

430 - Calories
21.5g - Fat
21.1g - Carbs
36.3g - Protein
4.6g - Sugars

Ingredients

- 5 cups vegetable broth
- 1 cup parsnip, chopped
- 1/2 cup celery stalk, chopped
- 1 cup turnip, peeled and sliced
- 1 ½ pounds pork ribs
- 1/2 teaspoon paprika
- 1/4 teaspoon black pepper, ground
- 1/2 tablespoon sea salt
- 1/2 cup celery rib, finely chopped
- 2 potatoes, peeled and diced
- 1 cup carrots, trimmed and sliced
- 2 cups greens, diced

Directions

1. Press the "SOUP/STEW" key. Simply add all the ingredients, minus the greens, to your Power Pressure Cooker XL.
2. Place the lid on the Power Pressure Cooker XL, lock the lid and switch the pressure release valve to closed.
3. Now, cook approximately 35 minutes. When the steam is released, open your Power Pressure Cooker XL. Add the greens and stir well until they're wilted. Bon appétit!

BEEF

61. Tomato Cabbage Rolls

White rice gives a wonderful texture to these cabbage rolls that will welcome you home when the days are cold and windy. However, you can make this recipe all year long.

Servings 6

Ready in about 55 minutes

NUTRITIONAL INFORMATION (Per Serving)

495 - Calories
7.9g - Fat
62.6g - Carbs
41.5g - Protein
8.2g - Sugars

Ingredients

- 10 cabbage leaves, blanched
- 1/2 teaspoon cayenne pepper
- 1 ½ pounds ground beef
- 15 ounces canned tomato sauce
- 1 tablespoon minced garlic
- 2 cups rice
- 5-6 whole black peppercorns, to taste
- 22 ounces canned tomatoes, diced
- 1/2 teaspoon sea salt, or more to taste
- 2 onions, chopped

Directions

1. Press the "CHICKEN/MEAT" key.
2. Combine the garlic, onions, beef, rice, tomato sauce, cayenne pepper, and salt in a mixing bowl; mix until everything is well combined.
3. Divide the meat mixture among the softened cabbage leaves. Roll the cabbage leaves up to form logs.
4. Place the rolls in your Power Pressure Cooker XL. Add the peppercorns and diced tomatoes.
5. Place the lid on the Power Pressure Cooker XL, lock the lid and switch the pressure release valve to closed. Now, cook for 50 minutes. Use a Quick release pressure.
6. When the steam is released, open your Power Pressure Cooker XL. Serve warm.

62. Herbed Pot Roast

This old-fashioned meal is easy to throw together into a revolutionary programmable Power Pressure Cooker XL. Feel free to pick another combo of spices. Mustard powder, marjoram and coriander work well, too.

Servings 8

Ready in about 50 minutes

NUTRITIONAL INFORMATION (Per Serving)

397 - Calories
13.8g - Fat
15.1g - Carbs
49.1g - Protein
3g - Sugars

Ingredients

- 1 pound red potatoes
- 1/3 cup red wine
- 1 tablespoon minced garlic
- 1/2 cup celery stalk, thinly sliced
- 1/2 cup parsnip, peeled and thinly sliced
- 1 teaspoon salt
- 1/4 teaspoon ground black pepper, to taste
- 2 ½ pounds chuck roast
- 2 tablespoons tomato paste
- 1 ½ cups beef stock
- 2 sprigs thyme
- 1 teaspoon rosemary
- 3 teaspoons canola oil
- 1 cup onions, thinly sliced
- 2 carrots, peeled and thinly sliced

Directions

1. Press the "CHICKEN/MEAT" key. Season the chuck roast with salt and ground black pepper.
2. Warm the canola oil in and sear the beef on all sides. Reserve the beef.
3. Add the vegetables to the Power Pressure Cooker XL and cook for about 5 minutes. Add the beef back to the Power Pressure Cooker XL, along with the rest of the above ingredients.
4. Place the lid on the Power Pressure Cooker XL, lock the lid and switch the pressure release valve to closed. Cook for 40 minutes.
5. Switch the pressure release valve to open. When the steam is released, open your Power Pressure Cooker XL. Bon appétit!

63. Delicious Beef Ribs with Vegetables

Root vegetables, tomato paste and beef ribs are natural allies in this rich family lunch that demands to be served with horseradish sauce and lots of cornbread.

Servings 8

Ready in about 55 minutes

NUTRITIONAL INFORMATION (Per Serving)

388 - Calories
11g - Fat
23.8g - Carbs
46.5g - Protein
5.5g - Sugars

Ingredients

- 1 ½ cups vegetable broth
- 1 ½ pounds potatoes, small
- 3 teaspoons vegetable oil
- 2 medium-sized red onions, chopped
- 2 bay leaves
- 1/4 cup tomato paste
- 2 sprigs rosemary
- 2 ½ pounds beef ribs, excess fat trimmed
- 1/2 pound carrots, peeled and thinly sliced
- 1/2 cup water
- 1/2 teaspoon freshly ground black pepper
- 1 teaspoon sea salt
- 1 cup parsnip, chopped
- 2 cloves garlic, peeled and finely minced

Directions

1. Choose the "CHICKEN/MEAT" function. Generously season the short ribs with sea salt and black pepper.
2. Warm the vegetable oil and brown the ribs on all sides. Reserve the ribs.
3. Add the parsnip, carrots, garlic, and onion; sauté for 5 more minutes.
4. Add the reserved browned ribs back to the Power Pressure Cooker XL; stir in the other ingredients.
5. Place the lid on the Power Pressure Cooker XL, lock the lid and switch the pressure release valve to closed. Cook for 45 minutes.
6. Once the timer reaches 0, the cooker will automatically switch to "KEEP WARM/CANCEL". Switch the pressure release valve to open. When the steam is completely released, remove the lid. Bon appétit!

64. Family Beef Stew

This classic dish may become your family favorite. You can make this wonderful stew a few days ahead because it freezes great as well.

Servings 6

Ready in about 35 minutes

NUTRITIONAL INFORMATION (Per Serving)

269 - Calories
9.6g - Fat
22.6g - Carbs
22.8g - Protein
6.4g - Sugars

Ingredients

- 10 ounces canned tomato sauce
- 1/2 cup water
- 1 teaspoon minced garlic
- 1 pound potatoes, diced
- 1/2 cup green bell pepper, sliced
- 1/2 cup red bell pepper, sliced
- 3 teaspoons vegetable oil
- 1 cup onions, slice into rings
- 2 teaspoons Worcestershire sauce
- 3 teaspoons cornstarch
- 1/2 pound carrots, chopped
- 2 ½ pounds beef chuck roast, cubed
- 2 ½ cups vegetable stock
- 1 teaspoon dried dill weed
- 1/2 teaspoon sea salt
- 1/4 teaspoon ground black pepper, to taste
- 1/2 teaspoon dried thyme

Directions

1. Press the "SOUP/STEW" key. Heat the oil and sear the meat.
2. Deglaze the Power Pressure Cooker XL with a splash of broth. Add the garlic and onion, and continue sautéing for an additional 1 ½ minutes. Press the "CANCEL" key.
3. Add the remaining ingredients. Place the lid on the Power Pressure Cooker XL, lock the lid and switch the pressure release valve to closed. Cook for 30 minutes.
4. Switch the pressure release valve to open. When the steam is completely released, remove the lid. Serve warm, dolloped with sour cream if desired.

65. Classic Pasta with Ground Beef Sauce

There is a creamier version of this classic pasta dish. Top each portion with a few tablespoons of grated yellow cheese if you want to bulk it up even more.

Servings 6

Ready in about 15 minutes

NUTRITIONAL INFORMATION (Per Serving)

319 - Calories
7.1g - Fat
34g - Carbs
29.1g - Protein
5g - Sugars

Ingredients

- 22 ounces dried egg noodles
- 1 teaspoon dried basil
- 1/4 teaspoon ground black pepper, or more to taste
- 1/2 teaspoon sea salt
- 1 teaspoon dried dill weed
- 1 ½ pounds tomato pasta sauce
- 2 onions, peeled and chopped
- 1 teaspoon smashed
- 1 pound ground beef

Directions

1. Choose the "CHICKEN/MEAT" function and brown the beef, stirring frequently. Press the "CANCEL" key.
2. Add the remaining ingredients. Choose the "BEANS/LENTILS" function. Place the lid on the Power Pressure Cooker XL, lock the lid and switch the pressure release valve to closed. Cook for 10 minutes.
3. Switch the pressure release valve to open. When the steam is completely released, remove the lid.
4. Divide among individual serving dishes and serve warm.

66. Festive Rump Roast

This super-easy pot roast cooks perfectly in your Power Pressure Cooker XL. Serve with a cold glass of quality beer.

Servings 8

Ready in about
1 hour 5 minutes

NUTRITIONAL
INFORMATION
(Per Serving)

330 - Calories
11.7g - Fat
1.6g - Carbs
54.1g - Protein
0.8g - Sugars

Ingredients

- 2 cups beef broth
- 1 cup onions, chopped
- 3 pounds rump roast
- 1 bay leaf
- 2 teaspoons olive oil
- 1/2 teaspoon ground black pepper, or more to taste
- 1 teaspoon salt

Directions

1. Choose the "CHICKEN/MEAT" function. Pat the rump roast dry and season with salt and black pepper.
2. Heat the oil and brown the meat on all sides. Remove your roast from the Power Pressure Cooker XL.
3. Now, add the onions, beef broth, and bay leaf; add the water to cover the ingredients. Add the roast back to the Power Pressure Cooker XL.
4. Place the lid on the Power Pressure Cooker XL, lock the lid and switch the pressure release valve to closed. Cook for 1 hour.
5. Switch the pressure release valve to open. When the steam is completely released, remove the lid.
6. Move the prepared roast to a serving platter. You can thicken the juices with a slurry of water and cornstarch.

67. Easiest Beef Stroganoff

You can substitute the sour cream with crème fraîche. What are the differences? Sour cream has a fat content of about 20% and it contains some thickeners. Crème fraîche has a fat content of about 30% and richer flavor.

Servings 6

Ready in about 35 minutes

NUTRITIONAL INFORMATION (Per Serving)

471 - Calories
21g - Fat
6.4g - Carbs
62.9g - Protein
2.8g - Sugars

Ingredients

- 2 ½ cups beef stock
- 1 ½ pounds mushrooms, sliced
- 2 ½ pounds beef sirloin, sliced
- 1 sprig dried rosemary
- 1 sprig dried thyme
- 2 tablespoons olive oil
- 1 cup red onion, peeled and finely chopped
- 1/2 cup sour cream
- 2 bay leaves

Directions

1. Choose the "CHICKEN/MEAT" function and heat the olive oil; sear the meat for 5 minutes.
2. Add the other ingredients, except for the sour cream.
3. Place the lid on the Power Pressure Cooker XL, lock the lid and switch the pressure release valve to closed. Cook for 25 minutes.
4. Switch the pressure release valve to open. When the steam is completely released, remove the lid.
5. Serve dolloped with sour cream. Enjoy!

68. Beef Ribs with Mushrooms

Here's one of the best winter-worthy dishes that is chock full of protein packed mushrooms, vegetables and aromatic seasonings. Sure, you don't have to wait for winter to try this recipe!

Servings 8

Ready in about 45 minutes

NUTRITIONAL INFORMATION (Per Serving)

296 - Calories
13.7g - Fat
6.8g - Carbs
35.7g - Protein
4.1g - Sugars

Ingredients
- 2 cups mushrooms, quartered
- 1 teaspoon minced garlic
- 1 cup carrots, peeled and thinly sliced
- 1/4 cup olive oil
- 2 ½ cups vegetable stock
- 1/4 cup tomato ketchup
- 2 sprigs rosemary
- 2 yellow onions, peeled and chopped
- 2 pounds beef ribs, excess fat trimmed
- 1/4 teaspoon ground black pepper
- 1/2 teaspoon salt

Directions
1. Choose the "CHICKEN/MEAT" function and heat the olive oil.
2. Now, season the short ribs with salt and ground black pepper. Brown your short ribs on all sides. Set the ribs aside.
3. Add the mushrooms, onion, carrots, and garlic to the Power Pressure Cooker XL; then, sauté for 5 minutes.
4. Next, add the ribs back to the Power Pressure Cooker XL along with the rest of the above ingredients. Cook for 35 minutes.
5. Switch the pressure release valve to open. When the steam is completely released, remove the lid. Transfer to a serving platter and enjoy!

69. Penne Pasta with Feta and Sausage

———————◠———————

Penne pasta and beef combine very well and this meal is attractive in appearance as well. Did you know that Feta cheese is much easier to digest than cow's milk cheeses?

Servings 6

———

Ready in about 25 minutes

———

NUTRITIONAL INFORMATION (Per Serving)

783 - Calories
40.4g - Fat
77.1g - Carbs
30.6g - Protein
14g - Sugars

Ingredients

- 1 ¼ pounds beef sausage
- 1/3 cup olives, pitted and sliced
- 3 cloves garlic, minced
- 20 ounces penne pasta
- 1/2 teaspoon dried basil
- 1/2 cup Feta cheese, crumbled
- 1/2 teaspoon ground black pepper, to your liking
- 1 teaspoon salt
- 2 ½ cups tomato paste
- 1/2 cup scallions, finely chopped

Directions

1. Choose the "CHICKEN/MEAT" function and brown the sausage for 5 minutes or until thoroughly cooked.
2. Add the scallions and garlic; sauté them for 5 more minutes or until fragrant and tender. Press the "CANCEL" key. Add the rest of the above ingredients, except for the Feta cheese.
3. Next, choose the "BEANS/LENTILS" function. Place the lid on the Power Pressure Cooker XL, lock the lid and switch the pressure release valve to closed; cook for 10 minutes.
4. Use a Quick release method, unlock, and open the Power Pressure Cooker XL. Garnish with the Feta cheese. Bon appétit!

70. Risotto with Beef Bacon and Cheese

This one-pot meal is best enjoyed warm and it also has the advantage of being simple to prepare. Feta cheese makes an excellent addition to this rich beef risotto.

Servings 4

Ready in about 30 minutes

NUTRITIONAL INFORMATION (Per Serving)

526 - Calories
17.5g - Fat
70.9g - Carbs
19g - Protein
2.5g - Sugars

Ingredients

- 4 cups chicken stock
- 1/2 cup Feta cheese, crumbled
- 1/4 teaspoon freshly ground black pepper, to your liking
- 1 teaspoon salt
- 1 teaspoon dried dill weed
- 1 cup leeks, chopped
- 3 garlic cloves, chopped
- 1 ¾ cups rice
- 1/2 tablespoon olive oil
- 2 tablespoons apple cider vinegar
- 2 sprigs dried thyme
- 1 teaspoon dried basil
- 1/2 teaspoon mustard powder
- 1 cup beef bacon, diced

Directions

1. Press the "RICE/RISOTTO" key and heat the oil; sauté the leeks and garlic until they are tender, about 5 minutes.
2. Stir in the bacon, rice, and chicken stock. Add the apple cider vinegar, thyme, basil, dill weed, and mustard powder. Season with salt and black pepper; stir to combine well.
3. Place the lid on the Power Pressure Cooker XL, lock the lid and switch the pressure release valve to closed; cook for 20 minutes.
4. Once the timer reaches 0, the Power Pressure Cooker XL will automatically switch to "KEEP WARM/ CANCEL". Switch the pressure release valve to open.
5. When the steam is completely released, remove the lid. Serve topped with crumbled Feta cheese. Bon appétit!

71. Delicious Country Stew

Here's a hearty and savory stew with the best aromatics that cooks to perfection every time in the Power Pressure Cooker XL. Yummy!

Servings 8

Ready in about 50 minutes

NUTRITIONAL INFORMATION (Per Serving)

297 - Calories
8.5g - Fat
15.5g - Carbs
37.8g - Protein
3.9g - Sugars

Ingredients

- 1/4 cup tomato paste
- 1 cup carrots, chopped
- 1/2 teaspoon celery seeds
- 1 cup celery stalks, chopped
- 1/2 teaspoon cumin powder
- 1/2 tablespoon lard
- 1/2 teaspoon red pepper flakes, crushed
- 1 teaspoon sea salt
- 1/4 teaspoon black pepper, ground
- 2 bay leaves
- 1 pound potatoes, chopped
- 1 teaspoon minced garlic
- 2 onions, finely chopped
- 2 pounds beef stew meat
- 3 teaspoons arrowroot flour
- 2 ½ cups beef bone broth

Directions

1. Choose the "CHICKEN/MEAT" function and sauté the beef, onion and garlic until the meat is no longer pink, approximately 5 minutes.
2. Add the remaining ingredients, except for the arrowroot flour.
3. Place the lid on the Power Pressure Cooker XL, lock the lid and switch the pressure release valve to closed; cook for 40 minutes.
4. Once the timer reaches 0, the Power Pressure Cooker XL will automatically switch to "KEEP WARM/CANCEL". Switch the pressure release valve to open.
5. When the steam is completely released, remove the lid.
6. To make the slurry, combine 1/4 of the cooking liquid with the arrowroot flour. Add the slurry back to the Power Pressure Cooker XL. Serve warm.

72. Pasta with Beef and Mushrooms

Here's a gorgeous autumn meal! For a little more kick, use jalapeno or another green chili pepper.

Servings 4

Ready in about 25 minutes

NUTRITIONAL INFORMATION (Per Serving)

428 - Calories
10.6g - Fat
49.9g - Carbs
35.6g - Protein
11.4g - Sugars

Ingredients

- 1 pound dried egg noodles
- 3/4 pound lean ground beef
- 2 cups mushrooms, chopped
- 3 cups tomato puree
- 1/2 teaspoon black pepper, ground
- 1 teaspoon salt
- 1/2 teaspoon dried basil leaves
- 1 teaspoon dried oregano
- 2 teaspoons olive oil
- 1 teaspoon minced garlic
- 1 cup onions, chopped

Directions

1. Choose the "RICE/RISOTTO" function and heat the oil; now, brown the ground beef for about 4 minutes.
2. Then, sauté the onions and garlic until they're tender, an additional 4 minutes. Press the "CANCEL" key.
3. Throw in the rest of the above ingredients. Choose the "BEANS/LENTILS" function.
4. Place the lid on the Power Pressure Cooker XL, lock the lid and switch the pressure release valve to closed; cook for 10 minutes.
5. Press the "CANCEL" key. Switch the pressure release valve to open. When the steam is released completely, remove the cooker's lid. Bon appétit!

73. Meat Dipping Sauce

This dipping sauce is perfect on a cold windy night when you and your guests need a rich and hearty snack. You can substitute chipotle peppers for minced habanero peppers.

Servings 12

Ready in about 25 minutes

NUTRITIONAL INFORMATION (Per Serving)

104 - Calories
4.7g - Fat
3.2g - Carbs
12g - Protein
0.4g - Sugars

Ingredients

- 1 pound ground meat
- 4 cloves garlic, sliced
- 1 can tomatoes, crushed
- 1/4 teaspoon ground black pepper, or more to taste
- 1/2 teaspoon salt
- 2 medium-sized shallots, chopped
- 1/2 teaspoon paprika
- 2 tablespoons vegetable oil
- 1 teaspoon minced chipotle peppers

Directions

1. Choose the "CHICKEN/MEAT" function and heat the vegetable oil. Now, sauté the shallots and garlic for 5 minutes. Stir in the chipotle pepper and the ground meat; cook until they are browned, an additional 5 minutes.
2. Add the tomatoes, paprika, salt, and ground black pepper.
3. Place the lid on the Power Pressure Cooker XL, lock the lid and switch the pressure release valve to closed; cook for 13 minutes.
4. Allow the pressure to release gradually and naturally. When the steam is released completely, remove the cooker's lid. Serve warm.

74. Rice with Mushrooms and Beef Roast

The next time you fancy a festive family lunch, try this mouth-watering rice recipe. You can substitute brown rice for white rice, if it is like that, reduce the cooking time to 6 minutes.

Servings 6

Ready in about 25 minutes

NUTRITIONAL INFORMATION (Per Serving)

498 - Calories
10.4g - Fat
81.6g - Carbs
18.9g - Protein
1.4g - Sugars

Ingredients

- 3 teaspoons vegetable oil
- 1 cup yellow onion, chopped
- 1 cup beef roast, cut into chunks
- 2 cups mushrooms, sliced
- 3 ¼ cups brown rice
- 1/2 teaspoon mustard seeds
- 1/2 teaspoon salt
- 1 teaspoon cayenne pepper
- 1/4 teaspoon ground black pepper, or more to taste
- 3 ½ cups water
- 1/2 teaspoon fennel seeds
- 1/2 cup celery stalk, thinly sliced

Directions

1. Choose the "RICE/RISOTTO" function. Press the "TIME ADJUSTMENT" key until you reach 18 minutes.
2. Simply throw all of the above ingredients into the Power Pressure Cooker XL. Lock the lid and switch the pressure release valve to closed.
3. Press the "CANCEL" key. Switch the pressure release valve to open. When the steam is released completely, remove the cooker's lid. Bon appétit!

75. Pasta with Beef and Tomato Sauce

Lean ground beef releases its juices during pressure cooking in this amazing pasta, flavored with dry aromatics. Try serving with some extra tomato ketchup and freshly grated Parmigiano Reggiano cheese.

Servings 6

Ready in about 25 minutes

NUTRITIONAL INFORMATION (Per Serving)

375 - Calories
9.4g - Fat
30.9g - Carbs
40.7g - Protein
4.6g - Sugars

Ingredients

- 2 cups fresh mushrooms, chopped
- 1 ½ pounds lean ground beef
- 20 ounces pound dry egg noodles
- 1 cup onions, chopped
- 1 teaspoon minced garlic
- 1 teaspoon dry basil
- 1 teaspoon dry dill weed
- 1/2 teaspoon ground black pepper, or more to taste
- 1 teaspoon sea salt
- 1 ½ pounds tomato paste

Directions

1. Choose the "RICE/RISOTTO" function and brown the beef for about 4 minutes, stirring continuously. Press the "CANCEL" key.
2. Add the other ingredients. Now, choose the "BEANS/LENTILS" function. Place the lid on the Power Pressure Cooker XL, lock the lid and switch the pressure release valve to closed.
3. Press the "TIME ADJUSTMENT" key until you reach 15 minutes. Switch the pressure release valve to open.
4. When the steam is completely released, remove the cooker's lid. Bon appétit!

VEGAN/ VEGETARIAN

76. Classic Winter Oatmeal

If you like oatmeal, and you also like savory breakfast, this winter meal may become one of your all-time favorites. As a bonus, oats are extremely healthy food and so easy to make!

Servings 4

Ready in about 15 minutes

NUTRITIONAL INFORMATION (Per Serving)

160 - Calories
5.5g - Fat
23g - Carbs
5.2g - Protein
0.6g - Sugars

Ingredients

- 1 ½ cups oats
- 1/2 teaspoon salt
- 3 cups water
- 1/2 cup fresh chopped scallions, for garnish
- 1/2 cup savory cashew cream, for garnish

Directions

1. Choose the "RICE/RISOTTO" function and put the inner pot into the Power Pressure Cooker XL.
2. Add the wire rack and 1½ cups of warm water to the inner pot.
3. Put the oats together with the remaining 1½ cups of water into a heat-proof bowl; sprinkle with salt. Lower the bowl onto the wire rack.
4. Place the lid on the Power Pressure Cooker XL, lock the lid and switch the pressure release valve to closed. Press the "TIME ADJUSTMENT" key until you reach 8 minutes.
5. Switch the pressure release valve to open. When the steam is completely released, remove the cooker's lid.
6. Divide the oatmeal among serving bowls; serve topped with cream and scallions. Enjoy!

77. Lemon and Blackberry Jam

———————❧———————

A twist on a childhood favorite, this jam is so quick to prepare. Enjoy with peanut butter and toast.

Servings 16

Ready in about 20 minutes

NUTRITIONAL INFORMATION (Per Serving)

211 - Calories
0g - Fat
56.3g - Carbs
0g - Protein
56.3g - Sugars

Ingredients
- 4 ½ cups caster sugar
- 2 tablespoons lemon juice
- 2 ½ tablespoons pectin powder
- 2 vanilla beans
- 3 ½ liquid pints fresh blackberries
- 1 cinnamon stick

Directions
1. Choose the "CHICKEN/MEAT" function.
2. Put the blackberries into your Power Pressure Cooker XL along with the pectin powder. Now, add the cinnamon stick, vanilla bean, and 2 cups of sugar; cook until the sugar dissolves.
3. Once the sugar has dissolved, allow the mixture to a boil for about 4 minutes. Add the remaining sugar and lemon juice. Then, ladle the jam into the 5 liquid pint jars.
4. Next, gently press the jam to release any excess air bubbles with a flexible spatula. Seal the prepared jars.
5. Place the jars in the Power Pressure Cooker XL; pour in the water. Put the lid on and press the "CANNING/PRESERVING" key; press the "TIME ADJUSTMENT" key until you reach 10 minutes.
6. Switch the pressure release valve to open. When the steam is completely released, remove the cooker's lid; carefully remove the jars with kitchen tongs or a jar lifter.

78. Creamed Green Lentil Soup

Did you know that wheat berries don't require an overnight soak? You can do that, but if you are in a hurry, boil them for 1 hour before pressure cooking.

Servings 6

Ready in about 20 minutes

NUTRITIONAL INFORMATION (Per Serving)

143 - Calories
5.1g - Fat
19.7g - Carbs
7.1g - Protein
6.5g - Sugars

Ingredients

- 2 cups green lentils
- 1 tablespoon curry paste
- 1 teaspoon minced garlic
- 1 cup coconut milk
- 3 cups vegetable broth
- 2 medium-sized yellow onions, peeled and diced
- 1/2 teaspoon ground black pepper, or more to taste
- 1 teaspoon salt
- 1 teaspoon dried dill weed
- 2 green Serrano peppers, thinly sliced

Directions

1. Press the "SOUP/STEW" key on your Power Pressure Cooker XL. Sauté the onions and garlic until tender or about 5 minutes.
2. You can add a splash of stock to prevent the mixture from sticking.
3. Add the curry paste and green Serrano pepper; stir to combine well. Pour in the coconut milk and broth. Now add the lentils, dill weed, salt and black pepper. Stir again.
4. Place the lid on the Power Pressure Cooker XL, lock the lid and switch the pressure release valve to closed.
5. Press the "TIME ADJUSTMENT" key until you reach 8 minutes. When the steam is completely released, remove the cooker's lid.
6. Switch the pressure release valve to open. Serve warm and enjoy!

79. Perfect Three-Bean Chili

It's almost embarrassing how easy this chili is! Beans fight free radicals, lower cholesterol, and prevent diabetes. Enjoy!

Servings 8

Ready in about 30 minutes

NUTRITIONAL INFORMATION (Per Serving)

122 - Calories
5.6g - Fat
13.6g - Carbs
5.7g - Protein
3.7g - Sugars

Ingredients

- 3 cups hot vegetable stock
- 1 teaspoon minced chili pepper
- 1/2 cup red bell pepper, seeded and thinly sliced
- 1 cup leeks, thinly sliced
- 1 teaspoon minced garlic
- 2 tablespoons vegetable oil
- 1 cup carrots, chopped into sticks
- 1 cup dried kidney beans, soaked, drained and rinsed
- 1 cup dried pinto beans, soaked, drained and rinsed
- 1 cup dried cannellini beans, soaked, drained and rinsed
- 1/4 teaspoon sea salt, to taste
- 1/2 teaspoon celery seeds
- 5-6 black peppercorns
- 1/2 teaspoon red pepper flakes, crushed
- 24 ounces canned diced tomatoes

Directions

1. Press the "BEANS/LENTILS" key and heat the oil; now, sauté the leeks and garlic for 6 minutes.
2. Now, stir in the other ingredients, except for the canned tomatoes. Place the lid on the Power Pressure Cooker XL, lock the lid and switch the pressure release valve to closed.
3. Press the "TIME ADJUSTMENT" key until you reach 20 minutes. When the steam is completely released, remove the cooker's lid. Switch the pressure release valve to open.
4. Add the tomatoes; stir until they are heated through. Serve topped with nutritional yeast if desired.

80. Oatmeal with Soy Sauce and Fried Eggs

Be inspired by amazing oats that will fuel you through hectic days! In this recipe, use steel-cut oats because they retain much of their shape after pressure cooking.

Servings 4

Ready in about 10 minutes

NUTRITIONAL INFORMATION
(Per Serving)

238 - Calories
13.1g - Fat
29.0g - Carbs
13.9g - Protein
4.7g - Sugars

Ingredients

- 1 ½ cup oats
- 1/2 teaspoon sea salt
- 2 ½ cups water
- 4 fried eggs
- 1/2 cup fresh chopped cilantro, for garnish
- 1/3 cup soy sauce

Directions

1. Choose the "RICE/RISOTTO" function and put the inner pot into the Power Pressure Cooker XL.
2. Add the wire rack and 1 cup of warm water to the inner pot. Drop the oats in a heat-proof bowl; add the remaining 1½ cups of water and sea salt. Lower the bowl onto the wire rack.
3. Place the lid on the Power Pressure Cooker XL, lock the lid and switch the pressure release valve to closed. Press the "TIME ADJUSTMENT" key until you reach 8 minutes.
4. Switch the pressure release valve to open. When the steam is completely released, remove the cooker's lid.
5. Add the soy sauce and give it a good stir.
6. Spoon the oatmeal into four serving bowls; top each oatmeal with a fried egg; scatter the chopped cilantro over the top. Enjoy!

81. Indian-Style Red Lentils

Who said lentils have to be boring? Red lentils, also known as masoor, are a staple of Indian cuisine, along with Garam masala, a spice mix that typically includes dalchini (cinnamon), clove, and cardamom.

Servings 6

Ready in about 25 minutes

NUTRITIONAL INFORMATION (Per Serving)

318 - Calories
8.1g - Fat
51.9g - Carbs
13.3g - Protein
3.3g - Sugars

Ingredients
- 4 ½ cups vegetable broth
- 1 ½ cups tomatoes, diced
- 1 ½ cups red lentils, rinsed
- 1 heaping teaspoon minced garlic
- 1 cup onions, diced
- 3 tablespoons grapeseed oil
- 1/4 teaspoon black pepper, or more to your liking
- 1 teaspoon cayenne pepper
- 1 teaspoon salt
- 2 pounds butternut squash, roughly chopped
- 2 teaspoons Garam masala
- 1/2 cup fresh chopped cilantro, for garnish

Directions
1. Press the "BEANS/LENTILS" key and heat the oil. Sauté the onions and garlic for 6 minutes.
2. Add the butternut squash, Garam masala, salt, black pepper, and cayenne pepper.
3. Continue cooking for an additional 4 minutes. Add the broth and lentils. Stir in the tomatoes.
4. Place the lid on the Power Pressure Cooker XL, lock the lid and switch the pressure release valve to closed. Press the "TIME ADJUSTMENT" key until you reach 8 minutes.
5. Switch the pressure release valve to open. When the steam is completely released, remove the cooker's lid.
6. Puree the soup with an immersion blender. Serve topped with fresh cilantro. Serve hot and enjoy!

82. Mushroom and Bean Soup

Delight your tummy with this appetizing and protein-packed soup! This recipe calls for fresh mushrooms such as raw portabella, morel, oysters, enoki, and so forth.

Servings 4

Ready in about 35 minutes

NUTRITIONAL INFORMATION (Per Serving)

145 - Calories
3.4g - Fat
20.3g - Carbs
12.1g - Protein
9.4g - Sugars

Ingredients
- 5 cups vegetable stock, preferably homemade
- 1 ¼ cups canned cannellini beans
- 4 cloves garlic, smashed
- 1 ½ cups onions, chopped
- 2 ½ cups canned tomatoes, crushed
- 1 cup celery stalks, chopped
- 1 ¼ pounds mushrooms, thinly sliced
- 1/4 teaspoon ground black pepper
- 1 teaspoon dried dill weed
- 1 teaspoon dried basil
- 1/2 teaspoon sea salt
- 1/2 cup parsnip, chopped
- 1 cup carrots, trimmed and thinly sliced

Directions
1. Press the "SOUP/STEW" key.
2. Simply throw all of the above ingredients into your Power Pressure Cooker XL; stir to combine well.
3. Place the lid on the Power Pressure Cooker XL, lock the lid and switch the pressure release valve to closed. Press the "TIME ADJUSTMENT" key until you reach for 30 minutes.
4. Press the "CANCEL" key. Switch the pressure release valve to open. When the steam is completely released, remove the cooker's lid. Serve right now!

83. Cauliflower and Broccoli Salad

Redefine your favorite comfort foods and make this crispy salad in no time. Scatter toasted pepitas over the salad.

Servings 6

Ready in about 15 minutes

NUTRITIONAL INFORMATION (Per Serving)

80 - Calories
4.5g - Fat
8.1g - Carbs
4.1g - Protein
2.8g - Sugars

Ingredients

For the Salad:
- 1 ½ cups water
- 1 pound broccoli, broken into florets
- 1 pound cauliflower, broken into florets
- 1 ½ cups carrots, thinly sliced

For the Vinaigrette:
- 1/2 tablespoon capers
- 3 teaspoons fresh orange juice
- 1/3 teaspoon ground black pepper
- 1 teaspoon salt
- 1/4 cup extra-virgin olive oil

Directions

1. Press the "FISH/VEGETABLES/STEAM" key.
2. Throw the carrots, cauliflower, broccoli and water into the Power Pressure Cooker XL.
3. Lock the lid and switch the pressure release valve to closed. Press the "TIME ADJUSTMENT" key until you reach 10 minutes.
4. Once the timer reaches 0, the Power Pressure Cooker XL will automatically switch to "KEEP WARM/ CANCEL". Switch the pressure release valve to open.
5. When the steam is completely released, remove the lid.
6. Meanwhile, mix all the ingredients for the vinaigrette. Strain out the vegetables and dress with the vinaigrette. Serve at once.

84. Chipotle Pumpkin Soup with Pecans

Hot, hot, hot! The recipe calls for chipotle pepper, but be sure to use the type of chili peppers that are best suited to the amount of heat you and your family are able to handle.

Servings 6

Ready in about 30 minutes

NUTRITIONAL INFORMATION (Per Serving)

120 - Calories
6g - Fat
13.8g - Carbs
4.6g - Protein
4.1g - Sugars

Ingredients

- 2 chipotle peppers, seeded and finely minced
- 2 ¼ cups vegetable stock
- 1 cup onions, peeled and chopped
- 2 ¼ cups water
- 1/3 cup pecans, pulsed
- 1/2 teaspoon cayenne pepper
- 1/4 teaspoon black pepper
- 1/2 teaspoon salt
- 1/2 pound potatoes, peeled and diced
- 1 cup apples, peeled, cored and diced
- 28 ounces canned pumpkin puree
- 1 heaping teaspoon smashed garlic
- 1/2 teaspoon ground allspice
- 2 tablespoons toasted pumpkin seeds, for garnish

Directions

1. Press the "SOUP/STEW" key and sauté the garlic and onion until they are browned, about 5 minutes.
2. Add the allspice, salt, cayenne pepper, black pepper, and the chipotle; cook for an additional 5 minutes. Add the potatoes, apples, pumpkin puree, ground pecans, water, and the stock.
3. Lock the lid and switch the pressure release valve to closed. Press the "TIME ADJUSTMENT" key until you reach 15 minutes.
4. Once the timer reaches 0, the Power Pressure Cooker XL will automatically switch to "KEEP WARM/CANCEL". Switch the pressure release valve to open.
5. When the steam is completely released, remove the lid.
6. Afterwards, transfer the soup to your food processor; pulse until completely smooth and creamy, working in batches. Serve warm, sprinkled with toasted pumpkin seeds.

85. Black Bean Soup

You'll be happy to know that these beans stay perfectly tender, unlike some other bean recipes you might have tried in the past.

Servings 4

Ready in about 25 minutes

NUTRITIONAL INFORMATION (Per Serving)

151 - Calories
6.6g - Fat
13.5g - Carbs
10.1g - Protein
2.8g - Sugars

Ingredients

- 5 cups vegetable stock
- 1/3 teaspoon chipotle powder
- 3 teaspoons vegetable oil
- 1/2 teaspoon ground black pepper
- 1/4 teaspoon cayenne pepper, or more to taste
- 1/2 teaspoon sea salt
- 3 cloves garlic, minced
- 2 cups dry black beans, soaked overnight
- 1 teaspoon dried basil leaves
- 1 cup onions, chopped
- 1 bay leaf
- 1/2 cup fresh chopped cilantro, for garnish

Directions

1. Press the "SOUP/STEW" key. Drain the black beans and reserve.
2. Next, warm the vegetable oil and sauté the onions and garlic for 3 minutes.
3. Add the chipotle powder, reserved beans, vegetable stock, bay leaves, and basil; season with salt, black pepper, and cayenne pepper; stir well.
4. Lock the lid and switch the pressure release valve to closed. Press the "TIME ADJUSTMENT" key until you reach 15 minutes.
5. Switch the pressure release valve to open. When the steam is completely released, remove the lid. Garnish with cilantro and serve.

86. Creamy Curry Lentil Soup

Curry lentils are comfort food in their purest form. You can use any type of lentils for this one, including brown, green and red.

Servings 6

Ready in about 20 minutes

NUTRITIONAL INFORMATION
(Per Serving)

75 - Calories
1.3g - Fat
12.3g - Carbs
5.7g - Protein
3.5g - Sugars

Ingredients

- 2 cups lentils
- 16 ounces canned coconut milk
- 1 heaping teaspoon minced garlic
- 1 cup red onions, diced
- 2 ½ cups vegetable stock
- 1 ½ tablespoons red curry paste
- 1/4 teaspoon ground black pepper, to taste
- 1 teaspoon salt
- 1 cup ripe tomatoes, chopped

Directions

1. Press the "SOUP/STEW" key and sauté the onions and garlic until beginning to brown, approximately 4 minutes. You can add a splash of stock to prevent the mixture from sticking.
2. Add the curry paste, and stir well. Pour in the coconut milk and stock. Now, add the lentils and tomatoes. Season with salt and black pepper. Stir again to combine well.
3. Lock the lid and switch the pressure release valve to closed. Press the "TIME ADJUSTMENT" key until you reach 10 minutes.
4. Switch the pressure release valve to open. When the steam is completely released, remove the lid. Bon appétit!

87. Three-Bean Vegan Chili

Whether as a great family lunch or a festive holiday fare, a chili with three types of beans is very likely to hit the spot. Serve with shredded vegan cheese or nutritional yeast if desired.

Servings 8

Ready in about 30 minutes

NUTRITIONAL INFORMATION (Per Serving)

146 - Calories
1.8g - Fat
25.3g - Carbs
9.2g - Protein
5.4g - Sugars

Ingredients

- 4 cups hot vegetable stock
- 1/2 teaspoon red pepper flakes, crushed
- 1 teaspoon minced chili pepper
- 30 ounces canned tomatoes, diced
- 1 cup carrots, chopped into sticks
- 1/2 cup green bell pepper, de-seeded and thinly sliced
- 3 cloves garlic, minced
- 1 cup leeks, thinly sliced
- 1/2 teaspoon coriander
- 1/2 teaspoon sea salt, to taste
- 1 teaspoon black peppercorns
- 1 cup dried pinto beans, soaked, drained and rinsed
- 1 cup dried cannellini beans, soaked, drained and rinsed
- 1 cup dried kidney beans, soaked, drained and rinsed
- 1 cup parsnip, chopped

Directions

1. Press the "BEANS/LENTILS" key and sauté the garlic and leeks for 6 minutes, adding a splash of vegetable stock as needed.
2. Now, stir in the other ingredients, except for the canned tomatoes. Lock the lid and switch the pressure release valve to closed. Press the "TIME ADJUSTMENT" key until you reach 20 minutes.
3. Switch the pressure release valve to open. When the steam is completely released, remove the lid. Add the tomatoes, stir, and cover until heated through. Bon appétit!

88. Potato-Leek Soup with Cremini Mushrooms

Cremini mushrooms, also known as Baby Portobello, have a deep savory flavor. This soup tastes great served with quinoa as a quick and nutritious dinner.

Servings 10

Ready in about 25 minutes

NUTRITIONAL INFORMATION (Per Serving)

133 - Calories
2.1g - Fat
25.1g - Carbs
4.7g - Protein
5.8g - Sugars

Ingredients

- 6 potatoes, peeled and cubed
- 2 cups cremini mushrooms, roughly chopped
- 1 cup leeks, trimmed and sliced
- 2 cups carrots, peeled and diced
- 1 cup parsnips, peeled and diced
- 1 teaspoon minced garlic
- 1 teaspoon fennel seeds
- 1/4 teaspoon black pepper, or more to taste
- 1/2 teaspoon salt
- 1/2 teaspoon marjoram
- 8 ½ cups water, boiling
- 2 ¼ cups coconut milk, unsweetened

Directions

1. Press the "SOUP/STEW" key and sauté the leeks and garlic approximately 6 minutes, adding boiling water as needed.
2. Add the rest of the above ingredients, except for the coconut milk.
3. Place the lid on the Power Pressure Cooker XL, lock the lid and switch the pressure release valve to closed. Cook for 10 minutes.
4. Switch the pressure release valve to open. When the steam is completely released, remove the lid. Pour in the coconut milk.
5. Mix your soup with an immersion blender for about 3 minutes. Adjust the seasonings, and serve warm, topped with nutritional yeast if desired.

89. Basmati Rice and Orange Salad

Using cooled rice is even better in this light and refreshing salad. You can substitute mint leaves for fresh chives or cilantro.

Servings 6

Ready in about 15 minutes + chilling time

NUTRITIONAL INFORMATION (Per Serving)

194 - Calories
3.2g - Fat
35g - Carbs
5.2g - Protein
2.5g - Sugars

Ingredients

- 2 ½ cups water
- 2 ½ cups basmati rice
- 2 tablespoons extra-virgin olive oil
- 1/2 cup orange, chopped
- 1 large bunch of spring onions, white and green parts, chopped
- 1/3 cup fresh mint, roughly chopped
- 1 cup bell peppers, cut into thin strips

Directions

1. Press the "RICE/RISOTTO" key. Rinse the basmati rice and add it to the Power Pressure Cooker XL. Pour in the water and place the lid on the Power Pressure Cooker XL.
2. Cook for 10 minutes. Switch the pressure release valve to open. When the steam is completely released, remove the lid.
3. Let the cooked rice cool completely and fluff with a fork. Transfer the prepared rice to a serving dish.
4. Add the remaining ingredients and stir to combine. Bon appétit!

90. Summer Quinoa Salad

Here is a simple and refreshing way to prepare and enjoy the super powerful and nutritious quinoa. Quinoa is loaded with vegan protein, manganese, fiber, and iron.

Servings 4

Ready in about 10 minutes + chilling time

NUTRITIONAL INFORMATION (Per Serving)

321 - Calories
5.2g - Fat
56.2g - Carbs
12.3g - Protein
1g - Sugars

Ingredients

- 2 cups uncooked quinoa, well rinsed
- 1/2 teaspoon ground white pepper, to taste
- A pinch of sea salt
- A pinch of ground cinnamon
- 3 cups water
- 1/2 teaspoon dried basil
- 1 cup thinly sliced cucumber
- 1 cup diced tomatoes

Directions

1. Press the "RICE/RISOTTO" key. Put the quinoa, water, cinnamon, salt, pepper, and basil into the Power Pressure Cooker XL.
2. Place the lid on the Power Pressure Cooker XL and set the cooking time to 2 minutes.
3. Then, use a Quick pressure release and carefully remove the lid.
4. Add the tomatoes and cucumber. Serve well chilled.

91. Winter Sweet Potato Soup

It's easy being vegan with this creamy soup! Sweet potatoes are a great source of fiber, vitamins, and minerals; coconut milk is also high in good-for-you minerals.

Servings 6

Ready in about 20 minutes

NUTRITIONAL INFORMATION (Per Serving)

168 - Calories
7.2g - Fat
21.5g - Carbs
5.3g - Protein
5.5g - Sugars

Ingredients

- 1 pound sweet potatoes, cubed
- 2 teaspoons fresh lemon juice
- 2 tablespoons canola oil
- 1/2 teaspoon cinnamon powder
- 1/4 teaspoon freshly grated nutmeg
- 3 tablespoons peanut butter
- 1 cup onions, roughly chopped
- 15 ounces coconut milk
- 2 ½ cups vegetable stock
- 3 cloves garlic, finely chopped
- 1/2 teaspoon black pepper, or more to taste
- 1 teaspoon sea salt
- 1 cup tomatoes, peeled, seeded and chopped

Directions

1. Press the "SOUP/STEW" key and heat the canola oil; sauté the garlic and onions, stirring frequently, until they are softened, about 5 minutes.
2. Throw in the other ingredients; stir to combine well.
3. Place the lid on the Power Pressure Cooker XL and set the cooking time to 6 minutes. Switch the pressure release valve to open.
4. When the steam is completely released, remove the cooker's lid. Puree the soup to your desired consistency, using an immersion blender. Serve in six individual bowls.

92. British-Style Beans

Rich in flavor and sinfully delicious, these beans could also be made with another type of dry beans. Serve hot, topped with roasted red peppers if desired.

Servings 8

Ready in about 30 minutes

NUTRITIONAL INFORMATION (Per Serving)

121 - Calories
0.7g - Fat
23.1g - Carbs
6.9g - Protein
4.4g - Sugars

Ingredients

- 2 ripe tomatoes, chopped
- 1/2 cup bell pepper, seeded and thinly sliced
- 1 heaping teaspoon minced garlic
- 1 cup celery stalk, chopped
- 1 tablespoon chili powder
- 1/2 teaspoon black pepper, or more to taste
- 1/2 teaspoon cayenne pepper
- 1/2 teaspoon coriander
- 1 teaspoon salt
- 1/2 teaspoon cumin powder
- 3 cups boiling water
- 2 cups dried black beans, soaked
- 1/2 cup dried red beans, soaked
- 1 cup carrots, chopped into sticks
- 2 medium-sized onions, peeled and chopped

Directions

1. Press the "BEANS/LENTILS" key. Drain and rinse the soaked beans.
2. Now, sauté the onions and garlic for about 6 minutes, adding a splash of boiling water as needed.
3. Add the remaining ingredients, except for the tomatoes.
4. Place the lid on the Power Pressure Cooker XL and set the cooking time to 15 minutes; lock the lid and switch the pressure release valve to closed.
5. Press the "CANCEL" key. Switch the pressure release valve to open.
6. When the steam is completely released, remove the cooker's lid. Stir in the tomatoes. Bon appétit!

93. Delectable Ginger Risotto with Almonds

As a common spice in Asian cuisine, ginger is among the healthiest foods in the world. It prevents heart diseases, fights bacterial infections and boosts immunity.

Servings 4

Ready in about 15 minutes

NUTRITIONAL INFORMATION (Per Serving)

354 - Calories
15.14g - Fat
65.1g - Carbs
9.9g - Protein
29g - Sugars

Ingredients

- 2 cups risotto rice
- A pinch of ground cinnamon
- A pinch of grated nutmeg
- 1 cup apples, cored and diced
- 1/3 cup candied ginger, diced
- 3 ½ cups almond milk
- 1/3 cup golden raisins
- 1/3 cup almonds, toasted and roughly chopped

Directions

1. Press the "RICE/RISOTTO" key; simply throw all the components, except the almonds, into the Power Pressure Cooker XL.
2. Place the lid on the Power Pressure Cooker XL; lock the lid and switch the pressure release valve to closed. Set the cooking time to 10 minutes
3. Press the "CANCEL" key. Switch the pressure release valve to open. When the steam is completely released, remove the cooker's lid.
4. Divide the risotto among individual bowls and serve garnished with the chopped and toasted almonds. Enjoy!

94. Refreshing Kidney Bean Salad

This kidney bean salad is amazing on its own, but you can also use it on your favorite tortilla or toss it with greens for a delicious and healthy lunch.

Servings 4

Ready in about 20 minutes

NUTRITIONAL INFORMATION (Per Serving)

124 - Calories
9.7g - Fat
6.6g - Carbs
2.6g - Protein
1.2g - Sugars

Ingredients

- 2 cups red kidney beans, soaked overnight
- 1 cup red onions, peeled and coarsely chopped
- 1 ½ tablespoons wine vinegar
- 2 bay leaves
- 5 cups water
- 1/4 teaspoon freshly cracked black pepper
- 1 teaspoon salt
- 1 teaspoon dried dill weed
- 1 teaspoon smashed garlic
- 1/4 cup extra-virgin olive oil
- 1/2 cup fresh cilantro, chopped

Directions

1. Press the "BEANS/LENTILS" key.
2. Add the water, kidney beans, and bay leaves to the inner pot of your Power Pressure Cooker XL.
3. Place the lid on the Power Pressure Cooker XL and lock the lid; switch the pressure release valve to closed. Set the cooking time to 15 minutes
4. Press the "CANCEL" key. Switch the pressure release valve to open. When the steam is completely released, remove the cooker's lid.
5. Drain the cooked beans and stir in the rest of the above ingredients. Stir to combine and serve chilled. Bon appétit!

95. Sweet Potato and Lentil Soup

Quick and tasty, this dish is perfect for your next family lunch. The combo of sweet potatoes, lentils, and canned beans has never tasted better!

Servings 6

Ready in about 25 minutes

NUTRITIONAL INFORMATION (Per Serving)

259 - Calories
6.1g - Fat
48.4g - Carbs
5.9g - Protein
13.8g - Sugars

Ingredients

- 2 pounds sweet potatoes, diced
- 20 ounces canned beans, drained and rinsed
- 3 ½ cups vegetable broth
- 1 can tomatoes, diced
- 2 tablespoons olive oil
- 2 tablespoons apple cider vinegar
- 1/2 teaspoon celery seeds
- 1 ¼ cups dried lentils
- 1/2 teaspoon ground black pepper
- 1/2 teaspoon sea salt
- 1 tablespoon chili powder
- 1/2 teaspoon cumin powder
- 1 cup onions, diced
- 1/2 tablespoon curry paste
- 1/4 cup fresh cilantro, roughly chopped
- 2 tablespoons parsley, roughly chopped
- 1 teaspoon minced garlic
- 10 ounces almond milk

Directions

1. Press the "SOUP/STEW" key and heat the olive oil; sauté the onions and garlic until tender, about 5 minutes.
2. Add the sweet potatoes and cook for a further 3 minutes. Throw all the remaining ingredients, minus the almond milk, into the Power Pressure Cooker XL.
3. Place the lid on the Power Pressure Cooker XL, lock the lid and switch the pressure release valve to closed.
4. Press the "TIME ADJUSTMENT" key until you reach 12 minutes. Switch the pressure release valve to open. When the steam is completely released, remove the cooker's lid.
5. Pour in the almond milk and stir well. Bon appétit!

SNACKS & APPETIZERS

96. Cold Appetizer with Beets and Walnuts

There's more than one way to cook beetroot. However, when you want to please your family in no time, pressure cooked tender and flavorsome beets are a must. Just like grandma used to make!

Servings 8

Ready in about 20 minutes

NUTRITIONAL INFORMATION (Per Serving)

144 - Calories
8.9g - Fat
22g - Carbs
3.4g - Protein
11.9g - Sugars

Ingredients

- 1 teaspoon cumin seeds
- 1/4 cup olive oil
- 3 teaspoons wine vinegar
- 1/2 teaspoon brown sugar
- 3 cups water
- 2 ½ pounds beets
- 1/4 teaspoon freshly ground black pepper, or more to taste
- 1/2 teaspoon sea salt
- 1/4 cup chopped walnuts

Directions

1. Press the "FISH/VEGETABLES/STEAM" key.
2. Add the beets and water to the inner pot of the Power Pressure Cooker XL.
3. Place the lid on the Power Pressure Cooker XL, lock the lid and switch the pressure release valve to closed.
4. Press the "TIME ADJUSTMENT" key until you reach 15 minutes. Press the "CANCEL" key. Switch the pressure release valve to open. When the steam is completely released, remove the cooker's lid.
5. Drain and rinse the beets and rub off the skins. Cut the beets into wedges. Transfer to a serving dish.
6. In a mixing bowl, combine the vinegar, cumin, brown sugar, salt, ground black pepper, and olive oil. Drizzle the mixture over the prepared beets. Scatter chopped walnuts over the beets and serve well-chilled. Bon appétit!

97. Easy Steamed Potatoes

Steamed potatoes are a cinch to make in the Power Pressure Cooker XL. With an addition of selected seasonings, this is a great, belly filling appetizer.

Servings 8

Ready in about 15 minutes

NUTRITIONAL INFORMATION (Per Serving)

117 - Calories
0.2g - Fat
26.7g - Carbs
2.9g - Protein
2g - Sugars

Ingredients

- 3/4 cup water
- 3 pounds potatoes, peeled and quartered
- 1 teaspoon salt
- 1/2 teaspoon freshly ground black pepper
- 1 teaspoon cayenne pepper

Directions

1. Press the "FISH/VEGETABLES/STEAM" key.
2. Insert the wire rack in the Power Pressure Cooker XL. Add the potatoes and water to the inner pot of the Power Pressure Cooker XL.
3. Place the lid on the Power Pressure Cooker XL, lock the lid and switch the pressure release valve to closed. Press the "TIME ADJUSTMENT" key until you reach 8 minutes
4. Press the "CANCEL" key. Switch the pressure release valve to open. When the steam is completely released, remove the cooker's lid.
5. Season the potatoes and serve immediately. Bon appétit!

98. Carrot Sticks with Pine Nuts

Carrot sticks are a dangerously addictive snack! Pine nuts are a great addition to this healthy, make-ahead dish.

Servings 8

Ready in about 15 minutes

NUTRITIONAL INFORMATION (Per Serving)

161 - Calories
9.7g - Fat
17.7g - Carbs
2g - Protein
8.8g - Sugars

Ingredients

- 1/4 cup sesame oil
- 1/4 teaspoon sea salt, or more to taste
- 1/2 teaspoon brown sugar
- 3 ½ cups water
- 3 pounds carrots, cut into matchsticks
- 2 teaspoons fresh orange juice
- 1/4 cup balsamic vinegar
- 1/4 cup pine nuts

Directions

1. Press the "FISH/VEGETABLES/STEAM" key. Add the carrot sticks and water to the Power Pressure Cooker XL.
2. Place the lid on the Power Pressure Cooker XL, lock the lid and switch the pressure release valve to closed. Press the "TIME ADJUSTMENT" key until you reach 5 minutes.
3. Press the "CANCEL" key. Switch the pressure release valve to open. When the steam is completely released, remove the cooker's lid.
4. Drain and rinse the carrots.
5. Then, make the vinaigrette. Combine the balsamic vinegar, fresh orange juice, sugar, salt, and sesame oil.
6. Drizzle the vinaigrette over the prepared carrots. Sprinkle with pine nuts and serve.

99. Winter Beef Dipping Sauce

Need something to pair with your favorite dippers such as pita wedges, veggie sticks, and tortilla chips? This meat dipping sauce will fit the bill!

Servings 10

Ready in about 25 minutes

NUTRITIONAL INFORMATION (Per Serving)

123 - Calories
5.8g - Fat
3.1g - Carbs
14.3g - Protein
1.2g - Sugars

Ingredients
- 1 pound ground beef
- 1 cup ripe tomato, chopped
- 1/2 teaspoon cayenne pepper
- 1 teaspoon salt
- 1 teaspoon dried thyme
- 1/2 teaspoon dried basil
- 1/4 teaspoon ground black pepper, or more to taste
- 1 teaspoon dried oregano
- 2 tablespoons canola oil
- 4 cloves garlic, sliced
- 1 ½ tablespoons arrowroot
- 1 ½ cups white onion, finely chopped

Directions
1. Press the "CHICKEN/MEAT" key and heat the oil. Stir in the ground meat and cook for 6 minutes, until the meat is no longer pink.
2. Add the other ingredients and stir until everything is well combined.
3. Place the lid on the Power Pressure Cooker XL, lock the lid and switch the pressure release valve to closed. Cook for 15 minutes.
4. Press the "CANCEL" key. Switch the pressure release valve to open. When the steam is completely released, remove the cooker's lid. Bon appétit!

100. Mediterranean Tomato Dip

One of the best ways to make sure you will enjoy your party is to serve a multitude of make-ahead snacks. You can make this dipping sauce a day ahead. Serve with bread sticks and enjoy!

Servings 12

Ready in about 20 minutes

NUTRITIONAL INFORMATION (Per Serving)

45 - Calories
1.6g - Fat
6.7g - Carbs
1.7g - Protein
4g - Sugars

Ingredients

- 4 cloves garlic, crushed
- 1/2 cup fresh basil leaves
- 1/4 teaspoon ground black pepper, to taste
- 1/2 teaspoon salt
- 1 cup carrots, chopped
- 1/3 cup olives, pitted and sliced
- 3/4 cup water
- 1/2 cup onions, peeled and chopped
- 3 teaspoons olive oil
- 25 ounces canned crushed tomatoes

Directions

1. Press the "SOUP/STEW" key and heat the olive oil. Now, sauté the garlic and onions until they are tender.
2. Add the carrots and basil leaves. Pour in the crushed tomatoes, olives, and the water. Season with salt and black pepper.
3. Place the lid on the Power Pressure Cooker XL, lock the lid and switch the pressure release valve to closed. Cook for 15 minutes.
4. Press the "CANCEL" key. Switch the pressure release valve to open. When the steam is completely released, remove the cooker's lid. Bon appétit!

101. Quick and Easy Potato Appetizer

Need last minute appetizer for your next dinner party?
Potatoes are always a good idea! This meal is so simple to
make and contains rich flavors of butter and garlic

6

**Ready in about
20 minutes**

**NUTRITIONAL
INFORMATION**
(Per Serving)

175 - Calories
7.8g - Fat
24.4g - Carbs
2.8g - Protein
1.8g - Sugars

Ingredients

- 1/2 stick butter, melted
- 2 pounds potatoes, peeled and quartered
- 1 cup water
- 1 teaspoon salt
- 1/2 teaspoon paprika
- 1/4 teaspoon ground black pepper
- 1 tablespoon garlic, finely minced

Directions

1. Press the "SOUP/STEW" key. Place the wire rack on the bottom of the inner pot of the Power Pressure Cooker XL; pour in the water.
2. Add the potatoes and the garlic to the Power Pressure Cooker XL. Place the lid on the Power Pressure Cooker XL, lock the lid and switch the pressure release valve to closed. Cook for 10 minutes.
3. Press the "CANCEL" key. Switch the pressure release valve to open. When the steam is completely released, remove the cooker's lid; taste the potatoes for doneness.
4. Transfer the prepared potatoes to a large-sized serving bowl. Toss them with the butter, paprika, salt, and black pepper. Bon appétit!

102. Buttery Acorn Squash

Did you know that acorn squash may help boost your immune system, improve vision health, and regulate blood pressure?

Servings 6

Ready in about 15 minutes

NUTRITIONAL INFORMATION (Per Serving)

167 - Calories
15.4g - Fat
8.1g - Carbs
0.8g - Protein
0g - Sugars

Ingredients

- 1 cup water
- 1 teaspoon baking soda
- 1/2 teaspoon sea salt
- 1/4 teaspoon freshly cracked black pepper
- 1/2 cup butter, melted
- 1 pound acorn squash, halved
- 1/4 teaspoon ground cinnamon
- 2 tablespoons apple cider vinegar

Directions

1. Press the "FISH/VEGETABLES/STEAM" key. Add the water and acorn squash to the Power Pressure Cooker XL.
2. Drizzle the squash with the apple cider vinegar. Add the remaining ingredients.
3. Place the lid on the Power Pressure Cooker XL, lock the lid and switch the pressure release valve to closed. Cook for 10 minutes.
4. Press the "CANCEL" key. Switch the pressure release valve to open. When the steam is completely released, remove the cooker's lid
5. Arrange the squash on a serving platter and serve.

103. Favorite Artichoke and Spinach Dip

Eating a diet rich in vegetables may help keep your body healthy and strong. Artichokes are an excellent source of dietary fiber, vitamins A and K, magnesium, phosphorus, and calcium.

Servings 12

Ready in about 15 minutes

NUTRITIONAL INFORMATION (Per Serving)

113 - Calories
8.1g - Fat
8.1g - Carbs
3.7g - Protein
1.1g - Sugars

Ingredients

- 1 ½ cups Mozzarella cheese, shredded
- 1/2 teaspoon ground black pepper
- 1 teaspoon kosher salt
- 1/2 cup light mayonnaise
- 15 ounces artichoke hearts, roughly chopped
- 12 ounces frozen spinach, thawed, drained and chopped
- 1 cup sour cream

Directions

1. Press the "FISH/VEGETABLES/STEAM" key.
2. Set a wire rack in the Power Pressure Cooker XL. Add all the ingredients to a baking dish; stir to combine well. Then, cover the baking dish with a piece of foil.
3. Lower the baking dish onto the wire rack.
4. Place the lid on the Power Pressure Cooker XL, lock the lid and switch the pressure release valve to closed. Cook for 11 minutes.
5. Press the "CANCEL" key. Switch the pressure release valve to open. When the steam is completely released, remove the cooker's lid
6. Serve warm with your favorite crackers. Enjoy!

104. Two-Pepper Tomato Dip

Here's a great addition to your holiday party! This rich, vegan dip is simply delicious; plum tomatoes, Mediterranean herbs and vegetables make a great blend.

Servings 8

Ready in about 20 minutes

NUTRITIONAL INFORMATION (Per Serving)

84 - Calories
5.4g - Fat
9.3g - Carbs
1.2g - Protein
5.9g - Sugars

Ingredients

- 1 cup carrot, chopped
- 1/2 teaspoon sea salt
- 1 pound plum tomatoes, peeled, cored and sliced
- 2 tablespoons brown sugar
- 1 teaspoon seeded and chopped Serrano pepper
- 1/2 cup shallot, diced
- 1/2 teaspoon dried basil
- 1 cup red bell pepper, seeded and chopped
- 1/4 teaspoon ground black pepper, or more to taste
- 3 tablespoons olive oil
- 1 sprig dried rosemary
- 1 cup water

Directions

1. Press the "SOUP/STEW" key and heat the olive oil; then, sauté the bell pepper, Serrano pepper, carrot, shallot, and tomatoes. Sauté for about 4 minutes, until the vegetables are softened.
2. Stir in the tomatoes, water, brown sugar, salt, black pepper, rosemary, and basil.
3. Place the lid on the Power Pressure Cooker XL, lock the lid and switch the pressure release valve to closed. Cook for 10 minutes.
4. Press the "CANCEL" key. Switch the pressure release valve to open. When the steam is completely released, remove the cooker's lid. Bon appétit!

105. Green Bean Delight

Green beans can help reduce the risk of diabetes, colon cancer and heart disease. This amazing appetizer tastes best when served right away.

Servings 6

Ready in about 15 minutes

NUTRITIONAL INFORMATION (Per Serving)

65 - Calories
1.4g - Fat
12.7g - Carbs
3.2g - Protein
2.6g - Sugars

Ingredients

- 1 ½ tablespoons bouillon cube
- 1/2 cup water
- 2 pounds green beans
- 1/2 tablespoon olive oil
- 4 garlic cloves, minced
- 1 cup green onions, minced

Directions

1. Press the "FISH/VEGETABLES/STEAM" key.
2. Add all of the above ingredients to the Power Pressure Cooker XL.
3. Place the lid on the Power Pressure Cooker XL, lock the lid and switch the pressure release valve to closed. Cook for 5 minutes.
4. Press the "CANCEL" key. Switch the pressure release valve to open. When the steam is completely released, remove the cooker's lid. Transfer to a serving platter and serve.

106. Black Bean Dip

Throw a few ingredients into your Power Pressure Cooker XL and make one of the most popular dipping sauces. What could be simpler?

Servings 12

Ready in about 30 minutes

NUTRITIONAL INFORMATION (Per Serving)

238 - Calories
5.1g - Fat
37.3g - Carbs
12.6g - Protein
2g - Sugars

Ingredients

- 1/4 cup olive oil
- A pinch of black pepper, freshly ground
- 1/2 teaspoon salt
- 1 cup tomatoes, chopped
- 1 ½ teaspoons red chili powder
- 3 garlic cloves, minced
- 1 cup red onion, finely chopped
- 1 sprig coriander leaves, finely minced
- 1 ½ pounds black beans, soaked overnight
- 1 ½ tablespoons Garam masala powder

Directions

1. Choose the "BEANS/LENTILS" function.
2. Add the black beans to the Power Pressure Cooker XL; cook until tender. Place the lid on the Power Pressure Cooker XL, lock the lid and switch the pressure release valve to closed. Cook for 15 minutes.
3. In the meantime, heat the olive oil in a nonstick skillet. Then, sauté the onions, garlic, and tomatoes for about 5 minutes. Then, add the red chili powder, Garam masala, coriander, salt, and black pepper; continue sautéing for 5 minutes.
4. Press the "CANCEL" key. Switch the pressure release valve to open. When the steam is completely released, remove the cooker's lid.
5. Now, transfer the sautéed mixture to the Power Pressure Cooker XL.
6. Then, blend the bean mixture in a food processor, working in batches. Serve with your favorite dippers.

107. Cheesy Corn on the Cob

Whether as a great snack or a light dinner, a healthy corn on the cob sprinkled with seasonings and freshly grated Parmesan is very likely to hit the spot.

Servings 6

Ready in about 5 minutes

NUTRITIONAL INFORMATION (Per Serving)

229 - Calories
5.1g - Fat
38.7g - Carbs
12g - Protein
6.7g - Sugars

Ingredients

- 1 tablespoon sea salt
- 8 ears of corn, husked, halved crosswise
- 1 cup freshly grated Parmesan cheese

Directions

1. Press the "FISH/VEGETABLES/STEAM" key. Set the wire rack in your Power Pressure Cooker XL.
2. Pour 1 cup of water into the base of the Power Pressure Cooker XL. Arrange the ears of corn on the wire rack.
3. Place the lid on the Power Pressure Cooker XL, lock the lid and switch the pressure release valve to closed. Cook for 4 minutes.
4. Press the "CANCEL" key. Switch the pressure release valve to open. When the steam is completely released, remove the cooker's lid. Sprinkle with salt and Parmesan cheese.

108. Famous Sweet Potato Snack

This is a complete treat for your guests! Sweet potatoes are loaded with antioxidants, anti-inflammatory nutrients and beta-carotene.

Servings 6

Ready in about
20 minutes

NUTRITIONAL
INFORMATION
(Per Serving)

219 - Calories
4.8g - Fat
42.3g - Carbs
2.4g - Protein
0.8g - Sugars

Ingredients

• 2 pounds sweet potatoes
• 1/2 teaspoon ground black pepper
• 1/2 teaspoon sea salt
• 1/2 teaspoon dried dill weed
• 2 tablespoons sesame oil
• 1/4 teaspoon paprika
• 1 ½ cups boiling water

Directions

1. Press the "SOUP/STEW" key. Place the wire rack on the bottom of the Power Pressure Cooker XL.
2. Pour in the boiling water. Next, drizzle the sweet potatoes with the sesame oil; wrap them in a piece of aluminum foil. Arrange the sweet potatoes on the wire rack.
3. Place the lid on the Power Pressure Cooker XL, lock the lid and switch the pressure release valve to closed. Cook for 11 minutes.
4. Press the "CANCEL" key. Switch the pressure release valve to open. When the steam is completely released, remove the cooker's lid.
5. Add the seasonings and serve immediately.

109. Yellow Wax Beans with Sesame Seeds

Fresh wax beans are low in calories and high in vitamins and minerals. They taste great mixed with sesame oil, leeks and garlic.

Servings 6

Ready in about
5 minutes
+ chilling time

NUTRITIONAL
INFORMATION
(Per Serving)

84 - Calories
4.7g - Fat
8.7g - Carbs
2.5g - Protein
3.2g - Sugars

Ingredients

- 3 teaspoons sesame oil
- 1 ½ cups vegetable stock
- 1 cup leeks, white parts only, minced
- 2 pounds yellow wax beans
- 3 garlic cloves, minced
- 3 tablespoons toasted sesame seeds

Directions

1. Press the "FISH/VEGETABLES/STEAM" key. Add all of the above ingredients, except for the sesame seeds, to the Power Pressure Cooker XL.
2. Place the lid on the Power Pressure Cooker XL, lock the lid and switch the pressure release valve to closed. Cook for 3 minutes.
3. Press the "CANCEL" key. Switch the pressure release valve to open. When the steam is completely released, remove the cooker's lid.
4. Serve chilled and sprinkled with sesame seeds.

110. Roasted Winter Squash with Sage

Here is a simple and nutritious way to prepare and enjoy the super powerful winter squash. You can substitute ground cloves for ground allspice.

Servings 8

Ready in about 15 minutes

NUTRITIONAL INFORMATION (Per Serving)

47 - Calories
0.3g - Fat
11.9g - Carbs
0.9g - Protein
0g - Sugars

Ingredients

- 2 teaspoons avocado oil
- 2 pounds winter squash, halved
- 1/4 teaspoon ground cloves
- 1/2 cup fresh sage leaves
- 1/2 teaspoon sea salt
- 1 cup water

Directions

1. Press the "FISH/VEGETABLES/STEAM" key.
2. Set the wire rack on the bottom of the Power Pressure Cooker XL. Pour in the water and arrange the squash on the wire rack.
3. Place the lid on the Power Pressure Cooker XL, lock the lid and switch the pressure release valve to closed. Cook for 10 minutes.
4. Meanwhile, melt the avocado oil in a saucepan over medium heat. Now, add the sage leaves and cook until they're crispy, approximately 1 minute.
5. Arrange the squash on a serving platter; sprinkle with crispy sage, sea salt, and ground cloves.

111. Cannellini Bean and Corn Dip

If you are feeling lazy, but still would rather prepare your own party dip instead of purchasing store-bought snacks, this recipe is here to help. Serve with veggie sticks or tortilla chips.

Servings 16

Ready in about 25 minutes

NUTRITIONAL INFORMATION (Per Serving)

137 - Calories
1.1g - Fat
24.3g - Carbs
9g - Protein
1.6g - Sugars

Ingredients

- 1 cup fresh corn kernels
- 3 garlic cloves, minced
- 1/3 cup tomato sauce
- 2 teaspoons olive oil
- 1/2 teaspoon cumin seeds
- 20 ounces canned cannellini beans, rinsed and drained
- 1/4 teaspoon ground black pepper, or more to taste
- 1/2 teaspoon paprika
- 1/2 teaspoon sea salt
- 1 ½ cups scallions, finely chopped

Directions

1. Press the "BEANS/LENTILS" key. Then, pour the can of beans into the Power Pressure Cooker XL.
2. Meanwhile, in a pan, cook the rest of the above ingredients until aromatic and tender.
3. Place the lid on the Power Pressure Cooker XL, lock the lid and switch the pressure release valve to closed. Cook for 15 minutes.
4. Once the timer reaches 0, the cooker will automatically switch to "KEEP WARM/CANCEL". Switch the pressure release valve to open. When the steam is completely released, remove the lid.
5. Next, add the sautéed mixture to the beans. Stir until everything is well combined.
6. Now, puree the mixture in a food processor or a blender, working in batches. Bon appétit!

112. Cilantro Lime Corn Snack

So quick to throw together, this tasty and corn snack is perfect served with white wine. Corn is a great source of antioxidants, dietary fiber, vitamins and minerals.

Servings 6

Ready in about 15 minutes

NUTRITIONAL INFORMATION (Per Serving)

216 - Calories
7.1g - Fat
38.8g - Carbs
6.7g - Protein
6.7g - Sugars

Ingredients

- 2 teaspoons lime juice
- 8 ears of corn, husked and halved crosswise
- 1/2 teaspoon salt
- 1/4 cup fresh cilantro, finely chopped
- 1/4 teaspoon ground black pepper
- 2 tablespoons melted coconut oil

Directions

1. Press the "FISH/VEGETABLES/STEAM" key. Set the wire rack in your Power Pressure Cooker XL; pour in 1 cup water.
2. Stack the ears of corn on the wire rack.
3. Place the lid on the Power Pressure Cooker XL, lock the lid and switch the pressure release valve to closed. Cook for 5 minutes.
4. Once the timer reaches 0, the cooker will automatically switch to "KEEP WARM/CANCEL". Switch the pressure release valve to open. When the steam is completely released, remove the lid.
5. Meanwhile, in a mixing dish, combine the remaining ingredients; mix to combine well. Toss the corn with this mixture and serve right away.

113. Vegan Spinach Dip

Here is a healthy and protein-rich vegan dip! You can play around with the amount of mayonnaise to match your preference.

Servings 12

Ready in about 15 minutes

NUTRITIONAL INFORMATION (Per Serving)

88 - Calories
7.3g - Fat
3.4g - Carbs
3.4g - Protein
0.3g - Sugars

Ingredients

- 1 ½ cups tofu
- 12 ounces frozen spinach, thawed
- 1 teaspoon dried dill weed
- 2 teaspoons fresh lemon juice
- 1/2 teaspoon ground black pepper
- 1 teaspoon salt
- 1 ¼ cups vegan mayonnaise
- 1 teaspoon grated lemon zest, for garnish

Directions

1. Press the "FISH/VEGETABLES/STEAM" key. Set the wire rack in your Power Pressure Cooker XL; pour in 1 cup of water.
2. Combine all the ingredients, except for the lemon zest, in a baking dish; give it a good stir. Wrap the baking dish with a piece of foil. Make a foil sling and lower the dish onto the rack.
3. Place the lid on the Power Pressure Cooker XL, lock the lid and switch the pressure release valve to closed. Cook for 8 minutes.
4. Once the timer reaches 0, the cooker will automatically switch to "KEEP WARM/CANCEL". Switch the pressure release valve to open. When the steam is completely released, remove the lid.
5. Sprinkle with lemon zest and serve.

114. Green Garlic Kale Hummus

Make the best hummus ever in a fraction of the time using a revolutionary easy-to-use electric pressure cooker. Serve with dippers of choice, such as crackers or veggie sticks.

Servings 12

Ready in about 25 minutes

NUTRITIONAL INFORMATION
(Per Serving)

169 - Calories
6.3g - Fat
22.2g - Carbs
7.4g - Protein
3.6g - Sugars

Ingredients

- 3 tablespoons tahini
- 1/4 teaspoon ground black pepper
- 1/2 teaspoon sea salt
- 2 cups chickpea
- 1 cup green garlic, minced
- 4 ½ cups water
- 2 tablespoons grapeseed oil
- 2 cups packed kale leaves

Directions

1. Press the "BEANS/LENTILS" key. Add the water and chickpea to the Power Pressure Cooker XL.
2. Place the lid on the Power Pressure Cooker XL, lock the lid and switch the pressure release valve to closed. Cook for 20 minutes.
3. Once the timer reaches 0, the cooker will automatically switch to "KEEP WARM/CANCEL". Switch the pressure release valve to open. When the steam is completely released, remove the lid.
4. Now drain the chickpeas; replace them to a food processor.
5. Add the kale, garlic, salt, black pepper, and tahini. Puree until creamy. Then, gradually pour the oil in a thin stream. Mix until everything is well incorporated.

115. Crispy Mustard Polenta Bites

Make these easy and healthy bites in no time. In this recipe, you can freely experiment with seasonings. Red pepper flakes, chipotle powder, dried rosemary and turmeric powder work well, too.

Servings 6

Ready in about 40 minutes

NUTRITIONAL INFORMATION (Per Serving)

180 - Calories
5g - Fat
30.7g - Carbs
3g - Protein
0.4g - Sugars

Ingredients

- 2 teaspoons Dijon mustard
- 1 ½ cups dry polenta
- 1/4 teaspoon ground white pepper, or more to taste
- 1 teaspoon kosher salt
- 1 teaspoon cayenne pepper
- 4 ½ cups water
- 1/2 teaspoon ground bay leaf
- 2 tablespoons coconut oil, at room temperature

Directions

1. Press the "CHICKEN/MEAT" key. Add the water, mustard, coconut oil, cayenne pepper, salt, and white pepper to the Power Pressure Cooker XL.
2. Press the "COOK TIME SELECTOR" key until the time reads 9 minutes. Slowly stir the polenta into the boiling liquid, stirring frequently. Add the ground bay leaf.
3. Place the lid on the Power Pressure Cooker XL, lock the lid and switch the pressure release valve to closed.
4. Once the timer reaches 0, the Power Pressure Cooker XL will automatically switch to "KEEP WARM/ CANCEL". Let the steam naturally release. When the steam is completely released, remove the cooker's lid.
5. Pour the polenta mixture into a cookie sheet. Refrigerate the polenta for about 30 minutes. Cut into bite-sized cubes and serve.

BEANS & GRAINS

116. Banana and Apple Rice Pudding

Light and delicious, this pudding is an ideal breakfast to munch on when you're on the go! If an apple and banana combo isn't your cup of tea, try adding your favorite fruits.

Servings 6

Ready in about 20 minutes

NUTRITIONAL INFORMATION (Per Serving)

519 - Calories
12.8g - Fat
88.4g - Carbs
13.2g - Protein
35.6g - Sugars

Ingredients

- 3 eggs
- 1 cup brown sugar
- 2 cups jasmine rice
- 1 ¼ cups half-and-half
- 1/3 cup apples, dried
- 1 cup bananas, dried
- 1/2 teaspoon ground cloves
- 1/2 teaspoon almond extract
- 1 teaspoon ground cinnamon
- 3 ½ cups whole milk
- 2 ¼ cups water

Directions

1. Press the "RICE/RISOTTO" key. Then, combine the jasmine rice, sugar, milk, and water in the inner pot of the Power Pressure Cooker XL.
2. Bring to a boil, stirring often, until the sugar is dissolved.
3. Place the lid on the Power Pressure Cooker XL, lock the lid and switch the pressure release valve to closed. Cook for 8 minutes.
4. Meanwhile, in a mixing bowl, whisk the eggs, half-and-half, cinnamon, cloves, almond extract.
5. Once the timer reaches 0, the cooker will automatically switch to "KEEP WARM/CANCEL". Switch the pressure release valve to open. When the steam is completely released, remove the lid.
6. Then, stir in the egg mixture, dried banana and dried apples. Serve warm or at room temperature.

117. Kidney Bean and Rice Salad

This is great, refreshing salad you can eat as a complete meal or as a side dish, no matter what the time of day. You can substitute kidney beans for black beans.

Servings 4

Ready in about 25 minutes

NUTRITIONAL INFORMATION (Per Serving)

441 - Calories
1.5g - Fat
88.5g - Carbs
17.9g - Protein
2.6g - Sugars

Ingredients

- 3 teaspoons avocado oil
- 1 ¼ cups kidney beans, soaked overnight
- 1 1/3 cups white rice, cooked
- 1/2 cup fresh cilantro, chopped
- 1 cup red onions, peeled and coarsely chopped
- 3 teaspoons balsamic vinegar
- 4 garlic cloves, smashed
- 1 tablespoon fresh orange juice
- 1 teaspoon orange zest, grated
- 1 teaspoon salt
- 1 teaspoon dried dill weed
- 1/2 teaspoon freshly cracked black pepper, to your liking
- 3 bay leaves
- 4 ¼ cups water

Directions

1. Press the "BEANS/LENTILS" key.
2. Add the water, kidney beans, and bay leaves to the inner pot of the Power Pressure Cooker XL. Place the lid on the Power Pressure Cooker XL, lock the lid and switch the pressure release valve to closed; cook for 20 minutes.
3. Press the "CANCEL" key. Switch the pressure release valve to open. When the steam is completely released, remove the cooker's lid.
4. Drain the cooked beans and stir in the other ingredients. Stir to combine and serve well chilled.

118. Friday Night Lasagna

This lasagna is perfectly suited for special occasions, giving your favorite family dish a chance to shine! Pick your favorite lasagna noodles, a pasta sauce and a combo of the best seasonings, arrange all ingredients in the inner pot, set back and enjoy!

Servings 6

Ready in about 1 hour

NUTRITIONAL INFORMATION (Per Serving)

351 - Calories
21g - Fat
31.8g - Carbs
9.5g - Protein
3.6g - Sugars

Ingredients
- 1 ¼ cups mushrooms, thinly sliced
- 1 ½ jars pasta sauce
- 1 teaspoon cayenne pepper
- 2 teaspoons dried basil
- 1 teaspoon dried rosemary
- 1 teaspoon red pepper flakes
- 1/2 teaspoon dried oregano
- 1/2 teaspoon sea salt
- 1 1/3 cups cream cheese
- 1/2 teaspoon ground black pepper
- 1 ½ packages prebaked lasagna noodles

Directions
1. Place two lasagna shells on the bottom of the inner pot of the Power Pressure Cooker XL.
2. Then, spread the pasta sauce. Place the layer of the cream cheese on it.
3. Top with the sliced fresh mushrooms. Sprinkle with some spices and herbs. Repeat the layers until you run out of ingredients.
4. Place the lid on the Power Pressure Cooker XL, lock the lid and switch the pressure release valve to closed.
5. Press the function key until you reach the bake setting; then press the "COOK TIME SELECTOR" key until you reach 50 minutes.
6. Press the "CANCEL" key. Switch the pressure release valve to open. When the steam is completely released, remove the cooker's lid. Bon appétit!

119. Cilantro Bean Purée

This recipe opens the door to endless possibilities. Serve this healthy, flavorful purée with pork chops, beef ribs or chicken wings.

Servings 6

Ready in about 25 minutes

NUTRITIONAL INFORMATION (Per Serving)

282 - Calories
3.2g - Fat
47.8g - Carbs
15.9g - Protein
2.5g - Sugars

Ingredients

- 2 ½ cups water
- 1 ½ teaspoons garlic powder
- 1 cup red onions, peeled and chopped
- 2 ¼ cups dry pinto beans, soaked
- 3 teaspoons vegetable oil
- 1/4 teaspoon black pepper
- 1 teaspoon chipotle powder
- 1/2 teaspoon red pepper flakes, crushed
- 1/2 teaspoon sea salt
- 1/2 cup fresh cilantro, roughly chopped

Directions

1. Press the "BEANS/LENTILS" key and heat the oil. Now, sauté the onions, cilantro, garlic powder, and chipotle powder.
2. Stir in the beans and the water. Season with black pepper, red pepper, and salt.
3. Place the lid on the Power Pressure Cooker XL, lock the lid and switch the pressure release valve to closed; cook for 20 minutes.
4. Press the "CANCEL" key. Switch the pressure release valve to open. When the steam is completely released, remove the cooker's lid.
5. Next, reserve two spoonfuls of beans. Puree the remaining beans using a potato masher. Season with black pepper, red pepper, and salt. Garnish with the reserved beans.

120. Pear and Coconut Dessert Risotto

This is a filling and comforting one-pot dish that is chock-full of wonderful aromas. Add 1-2 tablespoons of maple syrup if you want to satisfy your sweet tooth!

Servings 6

Ready in about 15 minutes

NUTRITIONAL INFORMATION (Per Serving)

544 - Calories
28.8g - Fat
67.8g - Carbs
7.4g - Protein
11.1g - Sugars

Ingredients

- 2 pears, cored and diced
- 1/2 teaspoon cardamom
- 1 cup coconut
- 2 ½ cups coconut milk
- 2 ½ cups water
- 2 tablespoons candied ginger, diced
- 2 cups white rice
- A pinch of ground cinnamon

Directions

1. Press the "RICE/RISOTTO" key. Throw all of the above ingredients into the Power Pressure Cooker XL.
2. Place the lid on the Power Pressure Cooker XL, lock the lid and switch the pressure release valve to closed; cook for 10 minutes.
3. Press the "CANCEL" key. Switch the pressure release valve to open. When the steam is completely released, remove the cooker's lid.
4. Serve at room temperature or well-chilled. Bon appétit!

121. Dates and Apricots Oatmeal Dessert

There are numerous benefits of eating oats. Oats are a whole-grain food with well-balanced nutrient composition. They are packed with antioxidants, soluble fiber, and minerals.

Servings 4

Ready in about
15 minutes

NUTRITIONAL
INFORMATION
(Per Serving)

456 - Calories
23.3g - Fat
62.5g - Carbs
6g - Protein
43.8g - Sugars

Ingredients

- 1 ½ cups steel-cut oats
- 2 ¼ cups water
- 1 ½ cups almond milk
- 3/4 cup brown sugar
- 6 fresh dates, pitted and sliced
- 8 apricots, pitted and halved
- 1 teaspoon vanilla paste
- 1/4 teaspoon ground cloves

Directions

1. Press the "RICE/RISOTTO" key.
2. Stir everything into the Power Pressure Cooker XL.
3. Place the lid on the Power Pressure Cooker XL, lock the lid and switch the pressure release valve to closed; cook for 8 minutes.
4. Press the "CANCEL" key. Switch the pressure release valve to open. When the steam is completely released, remove the cooker's lid. Serve well-chilled.

122. Beans with Mushrooms and Farro

Need something to go with your main course? Look no further! This bean and farro side dish is the perfect companion to stews, meat dishes and salads.

Servings 4

Ready in about 25 minutes

NUTRITIONAL INFORMATION (Per Serving)

251 - Calories
1.3g - Fat
46g - Carbs
17.1g - Protein
5.1g - Sugars

Ingredients

- 1/2 tablespoon shallot powder
- 1 teaspoon finely minced jalapeno pepper
- 1 tablespoon smashed garlic
- 3/4 cup farro
- 1 ¼ cups dried navy beans
- 4 green onions, chopped
- 1 cup tomatoes, diced
- 2 ½ cups mushrooms, thinly sliced

Directions

1. Press the "BEANS/LENTILS" key. Throw all of the above ingredients, except for the tomatoes, into the Power Pressure Cooker XL.
2. Place the lid on the Power Pressure Cooker XL, lock the lid and switch the pressure release valve to closed. Set the cooking time to 20 minutes.
3. Once the timer reaches 0, the cooker will automatically switch to "KEEP WARM". Press the "CANCEL" key and switch the pressure release valve to open.
4. When the steam is completely released, remove the cooker's lid. Add the diced tomatoes. Stir to combine well. Bon appétit!

123. Mexican-Style Bean and Corn Salad

Whether as a great starter or a light dinner, a healthy salad tossed with a flavorful vinaigrette is very likely to hit the spot. Enjoy this nutritious and delicious salad!

Servings 4

Ready in about 25 minutes + chilling time

NUTRITIONAL INFORMATION (Per Serving)

544 - Calories
26.4g - Fat
68.4g - Carbs
22.4g - Protein
3.8g - Sugars

Ingredients

- 1 teaspoon smashed garlic
- 1/2 teaspoon freshly cracked black pepper
- 1 teaspoon salt
- 2 tablespoons wine vinegar
- 1/2 cup fresh cilantro, chopped
- 1 teaspoon dried dill weed
- 1/4 teaspoon hot pepper sauce
- 1/4 teaspoon chili powder
- 1 tablespoon ground cumin
- 1/2 cup extra-virgin olive oil
- 2 cups cannellini beans, soaked overnight
- 4 ½ cups water
- 1 cup red onions, peeled and coarsely chopped

Directions

1. Press the "BEANS/LENTILS" key. Simply pour the water and cannellini beans in the inner pot of the Power Pressure Cooker XL.
2. Place the lid on the Power Pressure Cooker XL, lock the lid and switch the pressure release valve to closed. Set the cooking time to 20 minutes.
3. Once the timer reaches 0, the cooker will automatically switch to "KEEP WARM". Press the "CANCEL" key and switch the pressure release valve to open.
4. When the steam is completely released, remove the lid. Drain the cannellini beans; stir in the other ingredients. Serve well-chilled. Bon appétit!

124. Buttery Parmesan Risotto

Carnaroli is a short-grain rice that is perfect for any kind of risotto. Everybody will love this yummy and creamy dish!

Servings 4

Ready in about 20 minutes

NUTRITIONAL INFORMATION (Per Serving)

493 - Calories
13.2g - Fat
64.6g - Carbs
18g - Protein
3.5g - Sugars

Ingredients

- 1 ½ cups Carnaroli rice, uncooked
- 1 teaspoon grated lemon rind
- 2 ½ cups chicken broth
- 1 ½ cups sparkling white wine
- 2 tablespoons butter
- 1/2 teaspoon fresh thyme leaves
- 1 teaspoon sea salt
- 1/2 teaspoon freshly ground black pepper
- 2 garlic cloves, minced
- 2 onions, finely chopped
- 4 ounces Parmesan cheese, divided

Directions

1. Press the "RICE/RISOTTO" key and melt the butter. Now, sauté the onions for 3 minutes.
2. Add the garlic and sauté for 1 more minute, stirring frequently.
3. Stir in the rice and cook for a further 2 minutes. Pour in the sparkling white wine and the chicken broth and cook for 2 minutes longer.
4. Place the lid on the Power Pressure Cooker XL, lock the lid and switch the pressure release valve to closed; cook for 10 minutes.
5. Press the "CANCEL" key. Switch the pressure release valve to open. When the steam is completely released, remove the cooker's lid.
6. Sprinkle everything with the cheese, thyme, and lemon rind. Season with salt and black pepper and serve.

125. Super Creamy Rice Pudding

A creamy, fragrant and tender rice . . . Arborio rice is a short-grained, high-starch rice that cooks quick and easy in your Power Pressure Cooker XL. It takes over 30 minutes to make it in a traditional way, at the stove. Need we say more?

Servings 6

Ready in about 25 minutes

NUTRITIONAL INFORMATION (Per Serving)

322 - Calories
13.2g - Fat
40.4g - Carbs
8.8g - Protein
15.5g - Sugars

Ingredients

- 2 tablespoons butter
- 1/2 cup heavy cream
- 2 eggs plus 2 egg yolks, lightly beaten
- 1 tablespoon pure vanilla extract
- 1/4 teaspoon ground cinnamon
- 1 teaspoon almond extract
- 1/8 teaspoon salt
- 1 ¼ cups water
- 1/3 cup sugar
- 1 cup Arborio rice
- 1/8 teaspoon grated nutmeg
- 1 ¾ cups whole milk

Directions

1. Press the "RICE/RISOTTO" key and melt the butter.
2. Toast the rice for 2 minutes, stirring frequently. Next, add the milk, sugar, vanilla extract, almond extract, salt, nutmeg, ground cinnamon, and water. Cook the mixture for 2 minutes more or until heated through, stirring constantly.
3. Place the lid on the Power Pressure Cooker XL, lock the lid and switch the pressure release valve to closed; cook for 10 minutes.
4. Press the "CANCEL" key. Switch the pressure release valve to open. When the steam is completely released, remove the cooker's lid.
5. In a mixing dish, whisk the eggs, egg yolks, and heavy cream until smooth and frothy. Add about 2 cups of the hot pudding mixture to the egg mixture; add the mixture to the Power Pressure Cooker XL.
6. Afterwards, stir the pudding until it has thickened. Serve warm.

126. Mashed Garbanzo Beans

This is a delicious, high-protein dish that can be eaten as an appetizer or a side dish. Serve with a sparkling wine as an aperitif. In addition, garbanzo beans are loaded with antioxidants

Servings 6

Ready in about 20 minutes

NUTRITIONAL
INFORMATION
(Per Serving)

247 - Calories
6.2g - Fat
37g - Carbs
12.8g - Protein
6.3g - Sugars

Ingredients

- 1/2 tablespoon stone ground mustard
- 1 bay leaf
- 1 ¾ cups dried garbanzo beans
- 3 garlic cloves, finely minced
- 1/4 cup toasted pumpkin seeds, for garnish
- 1/2 cup cilantro
- Salt and pepper, to your liking

Directions

1. Press the "BEANS/LENTILS" key. Place the garbanzo beans and bay leaf in your Power Pressure Cooker XL.
2. Add the water to cover the beans.
3. Place the lid on the Power Pressure Cooker XL, lock the lid and switch the pressure release valve to closed; cook for 10 minutes.
4. Press the "CANCEL" key. Switch the pressure release valve to open. When the steam is completely released, remove the cooker's lid.
5. Drain and rinse the garbanzo beans; discard the bay leaf. Then, mash them with a fork, potato masher or pastry blender.
6. Add the minced garlic, cilantro, and mustard, salt and pepper. Adjust the seasonings. Serve sprinkled with the toasted pumpkin seeds. Enjoy!

127. Indian-Style Bean Dip

An easy to make dipping sauce that goes best with Indian starters and naan. You can add some extra Indian spices like turmeric, tejpat, tamarind, saffron, kokam and so forth.

Servings 12

Ready in about 25 minutes

NUTRITIONAL INFORMATION (Per Serving)

238 - Calories
4.9g - Fat
37.1g - Carbs
13.2g - Protein
2.2g - Sugars

Ingredients
- 1 heaping tablespoon coriander leaves, finely minced
- 1/2 tablespoon Garam masala powder
- 1 cup onions, finely chopped
- 1 ½ cups tomatoes, chopped
- 1/2 teaspoon cumin seeds
- 1/4 cup olive oil
- 1 ½ pounds kidney beans, soaked overnight
- 1 teaspoon fresh ginger, grated
- 1/4 teaspoon salt
- 1/2 teaspoon red chili powder
- 4 garlic cloves, minced

Directions
1. Press the "BEANS/LENTILS" key. Add the kidney beans to the Power Pressure Cooker XL. Add the water to cover the beans. Place the lid on the Power Pressure Cooker XL, lock the lid and switch the pressure release valve to closed; cook for 20 minutes.
2. Meanwhile, in a saucepan, heat the olive oil. Then, sauté the onions with the garlic, ginger, tomatoes, Garam masala, red chili powder, and the cumin seeds.
3. Press the "CANCEL" key. Switch the pressure release valve to open. When the steam is completely released, remove the cooker's lid.
4. Next, stir the sautéed mixture into your Power Pressure Cooker XL. Add the coriander leaves and salt.
5. Next, blend the bean mixture in a food processor; work with batches. Serve and enjoy!

128. Bread Pudding with Dried Apricots

Bread pudding is a comfort food that truly satisfies.
Don't throw stale bread away because you can make a
sophisticated, no-fuss family meal in no time!

Servings 6

Ready in about
25 minutes

NUTRITIONAL
INFORMATION
(Per Serving)

416 - Calories
19.9g - Fat
47.4g - Carbs
15g - Protein
18.8g - Sugars

Ingredients

- 4 eggs
- 1 ½ cups almond milk
- 1/2 teaspoon vanilla extract
- 8 slices stale bread, torn into bite-sized pieces
- 1/3 teaspoon grated nutmeg
- 1/3 cup sugar
- 1 ½ cups water
- 1 teaspoon almond extract
- 1/4 teaspoon salt
- 1/2 cup chopped dried apricot, for garnish

Directions

1. Press the "RICE/RISOTTO" key.
2. Lightly butter a baking dish. Throw the bread pieces into the bowl.
3. To make the custard, combine the almond milk, water, eggs, vanilla extract, almond extract, salt, sugar, and the nutmeg.
4. Pour the custard mixture over the bread pieces. Scatter the chopped apricots over the top. Cover tightly with a piece of foil that has been greased.
5. Place the wire rack in the inner pot of the Power Pressure Cooker XL. Pour in 2 cups of water. Secure the lid on your Power Pressure Cooker XL.
6. Press the "COOK TIME SELECTOR" to set for 18 minutes. Press the "CANCEL" key. Switch the pressure release valve to open. When the steam is completely released, remove the cooker's lid. Bon appétit!

129. Italian-Style Penne Pasta with Sausage

Did you know that wheat berries don't require an overnight soak? You can do that, but if you are in a hurry, boil them for 1 hour before pressure cooking.

Servings 4

Ready in about 15 minutes

NUTRITIONAL INFORMATION (Per Serving)

648 - Calories
16.9g - Fat
87g - Carbs
36.8g - Protein
13.1g - Sugars

Ingredients

- 1 ¼ pounds Italian sausage
- 1 teaspoon minced garlic
- 1 cup onion, diced
- 1 ½ cups Porcini mushrooms, thinly sliced
- 1 pound penne pasta
- 2 cups pasta sauce
- 3 cups water
- 1 cup Mozzarella cheese, shredded

Directions

1. Choose the "RICE/RISOTTO" function. Set the cooking time to 8 minutes.
2. Then, brown the Italian sausage along with the garlic, onions, and mushrooms. Cook until the vegetables are tender.
3. Add the penne pasta, pasta sauce, and water. Stir well with a large-sized spatula.
4. Place the lid on the Power Pressure Cooker XL, lock the lid and switch the pressure release valve to closed.
5. Once the timer reaches 0, the cooker will automatically switch to "KEEP WARM/CANCEL". When the steam is completely released, remove the lid.
6. Stir in the mozzarella cheese and serve.

130. Banana Cranberry Oatmeal

Thanks to its amazing technology, The Power Pressure Cooker XL will take your oatmeal from "blah" to "yippee"! In this recipe, you can substitute the cranberries for dried cherries.

Servings 4

Ready in about 15 minutes

NUTRITIONAL INFORMATION (Per Serving)

290 - Calories
5.4g - Fat
53.9g - Carbs
6.6g - Protein
21.9g - Sugars

Ingredients

- 1/3 cup sugar
- 1 teaspoon vanilla extract
- 1/4 teaspoon ground cloves
- 1/2 cup dried cranberries
- 1 cup ripe banana, chopped
- 1/8 teaspoon salt
- 1 cup steel-cut oats
- 1/4 cup whipped cream
- 2 ½ cups water

Directions

1. Choose the "RICE/RISOTTO" function.
2. Press the "TIME ADJUSTMENT" key and set the timer for 10 minutes.
3. Mix all of the above ingredients, except for the heavy cream, in your Power Pressure Cooker XL. Stir to combine well.
4. Place the lid on the Power Pressure Cooker XL, lock the lid and switch the pressure release valve to closed.
5. Once the timer reaches 0, the cooker will automatically switch to "KEEP WARM/CANCEL". When the steam is completely released, remove the lid.
6. Serve with the whipped cream.

131. Bulgur and Almond Porridge

Bulgur is a kind of wheat that is good for your digestion. It may protect your heart, fight diabetes, and help with weight loss. Bulgur wheat pairs deliciously with cardamom, anise star, and vanilla.

Servings 8

Ready in about 15 minutes

NUTRITIONAL INFORMATION (Per Serving)

177 - Calories
1.7g - Fat
38.9g - Carbs
4.8g - Protein
11.9g - Sugars

Ingredients

- 2 cups bulgur wheat
- 1/4 teaspoon freshly grated nutmeg
- 1/2 teaspoon ground cloves
- 1/2 teaspoon ground cinnamon
- 3 tablespoons toasted almonds, chopped
- 1/3 cup honey
- 6 cups water

Directions

1. Choose the "BEANS/LENTILS" function. Mix all the ingredients, the minus honey, in your Power Pressure Cooker XL.
2. Place the lid on the Power Pressure Cooker XL, lock the lid and switch the pressure release valve to closed. Cook for 10 minutes.
3. Once the timer reaches 0, the cooker will automatically switch to "KEEP WARM/CANCEL". When the steam is completely released, remove the lid.
4. Add the honey and stir well before serving. Bon appétit!

132. Smoky Winter Grits

Here's one of the easiest ways to cook perfect grits. So quick to throw together, grits go well with ham, shallots, and Parmesan cheese

Servings 6

Ready in about 30 minutes

NUTRITIONAL INFORMATION (Per Serving)

296 - Calories
19.2g - Fat
12.7g - Carbs
19.5g - Protein
0.7g - Sugars

Ingredients

- 1 cup quick-cooking grits
- 1/2 stick butter
- 3 eggs, whisked
- 1/2 teaspoon ground black pepper, to your liking
- 1 teaspoon sea salt
- 1 teaspoon smoked paprika
- 2 medium-sized shallots, chopped
- 10 ounces ham, chopped
- 1 cup Parmesan cheese, grated

Directions

1. Choose the "RICE/RISOTTO" function and warm the butter.
2. Now, brown the ham for 2 minutes and crumble it. Add the shallots, salt, black pepper, and the smoked paprika; cook for 3 more minutes, stirring frequently. Reserve the mixture.
3. In a saucepan, bring 3 cups of water to a boil. Whisk in the grits and cook, until thickened, about 6 minutes. Stir into the bowl with the ham mixture.
4. Stir in the eggs and the Parmesan cheese.
5. Place the wire rack in the Power Pressure Cooker XL; pour in 2 cups of water. Make the foil sling and butter the bottom and sides of a baking dish. Spread the mixture in the baking dish.
6. Place the lid on the Power Pressure Cooker XL, lock the lid and switch the pressure release valve to closed. Cook for 10 minutes.
7. Afterwards, press the "CANCEL" key. When the steam is completely released, remove the cooker's lid. Serve warm.

133. Honey Pecan Oatmeal

There is absolutely nothing a good oatmeal won't cure.
Add amazingly healthy pecans and honey, and delight your
family with something special!

Servings 4

**Ready in about
15 minutes**

**NUTRITIONAL
INFORMATION
(Per Serving)**

321 - Calories
22.8g - Fat
29.6g - Carbs
5.3g - Protein
18.7g - Sugars

Ingredients

- 1 ¼ cups steel-cut oats
- 1/4 cup honey
- 2 cups water
- 1/4 cup pecans, chopped
- 1/4 teaspoon kosher salt

Directions

1. Choose the "RICE/RISOTTO" function. Press the "TIME ADJUSTMENT" key and set the time to 10 minutes.
2. Add the water, oats, and salt to your Power Pressure Cooker XL. Stir to combine well.
3. Place the lid on the Power Pressure Cooker XL, lock the lid and switch the pressure release valve to closed.
4. While the oats are cooking, toast the pecans in a small-sized skillet.
5. Once the timer reaches 0, the cooker will automatically switch to "KEEP WARM/CANCEL".
6. When the steam is completely released, remove the lid. Afterwards, add honey and stir to combine well. Serve sprinkled with chopped pecans. Bon appétit!

134. Ham Bread Pudding with Swiss Cheese

This bread pudding will wow your guests! Serve with a spoonful of Greek-style yogurt for an extra special treat!

Servings 6

Ready in about 35 minutes

NUTRITIONAL INFORMATION (Per Serving)

499 - Calories
15.7g - Fat
64.6g - Carbs
24.1g - Protein
9.5g - Sugars

Ingredients

- 1 ½ pounds Hawaiian bread rolls, torn into pieces
- Nonstick cooking spray
- 2 cups milk
- 1/4 teaspoon ground black pepper, or more to taste
- 1/2 teaspoon salt
- 1 cup ham, chopped
- 1/2 tablespoon Dijon mustard
- 1/2 teaspoon brown sugar
- 4 eggs, at room temperature
- 4 green onions, chopped
- 4 ounces Swiss cheese, shredded

Directions

1. Choose the "CHICKEN/MEAT" function. Coat the inside of a soufflé dish with a nonstick cooking spray; set aside. Place the wire rack in your Power Pressure Cooker XL; pour in 2 cups of warm water.
2. Heat a cast-iron skillet over medium heat and cook the ham and green onions for 5 minutes. Transfer the ham-onion mixture to the soufflé dish; add the bread pieces.
3. In another bowl, whisk the eggs, Dijon mustard, milk, brown sugar, salt, and black pepper. Pour the egg mixture over the bread pieces; press with a spatula to submerge the bread pieces. Allow it to stand for 5 minutes.
4. Cover the baking dish with a piece of parchment paper; then seal with a piece of aluminum foil. Make the foil sling and lower the sealed dish onto the rack.
5. Press the "TIME ADJUSTMENT" key and set time to 20 minutes. Place the lid on the Power Pressure Cooker XL, lock the lid and switch the pressure release valve to closed.
6. Once the timer reaches 0, the cooker will automatically switch to "KEEP WARM/CANCEL".
7. When the steam is completely released, remove the lid. Serve at room temperature topped with shredded Swiss cheese.

135. Black Bean and Corn Dip

A combo of corn kernels and black beans is always a good idea. Serve with potato chips or veggie sticks for a memorable Super Bowl feast.

Servings 16

Ready in about 25 minutes

NUTRITIONAL INFORMATION
(Per Serving)

139 - Calories
3.4g - Fat
21.4g - Carbs
6.9g - Protein
1.5g - Sugars

Ingredients

- 1 cup fresh corn kernels
- 5 cups water
- 1 pound black beans, rinsed and drained
- 1 cup onion, finely chopped
- 1/2 teaspoon celery seeds
- 4 garlic cloves, minced
- 2 tablespoons canola oil
- 1/2 teaspoon sea salt
- 1/4 teaspoon ground black pepper, or more to your liking
- 1/2 teaspoon cumin seeds
- 1 cup mild picante sauce

Directions

1. Press the "BEANS/LENTILS" key. Then, empty the can of beans into your Power Pressure Cooker XL. Add the water.
2. Place the lid on the Power Pressure Cooker XL, lock the lid and switch the pressure release valve to closed. Cook your beans for 10 minutes.
3. Meanwhile, in a saucepan, cook the remaining ingredients for 5 minutes or until tender.
4. Once the timer reaches 0, the Power Pressure Cooker XL will automatically switch to "KEEP WARM/ CANCEL". Switch the pressure release valve to open.
5. When the steam is completely released, remove the cooker's lid. Throw in the sautéed mixture; stir to combine.
6. Now, pulse the mixture in your blender or a food processor, working in batches. Bon appétit!

DESSERTS

136. Classic Chocolate Pudding

When you're looking for just the right thing to serve for dessert, this chocolate pudding will fit the bill. You might need to make a double batch because it disappears almost as fast as you can make it!

Servings 6

Ready in about 20 minutes

NUTRITIONAL INFORMATION (Per Serving)

502 - Calories
32.7g - Fat
52.2g - Carbs
5.9g - Protein
45.4g - Sugars

Ingredients

- 7 tablespoons brown sugar
- 1 teaspoon almond extract
- 8 ounces semisweet chocolate, chopped
- 10 ounces dark chocolate, chopped
- 1/2 tablespoon vanilla extract
- 3 large-sized egg yolks, whisked
- 1 ¾ cups light cream
- 1/8 teaspoon salt

Directions

1. Press the "SOUP/STEW" key.
2. Place the chocolate and the sugar in a mixing dish. Warm the light cream in a pan over low heat.
3. Pour the warmed cream over the chocolate; whisk until the chocolate has melted. Add the yolks, almond extract, vanilla extract, and salt.
4. Pour the mixture into six heat-safe ramekins. Cover each ramekin with foil.
5. Set the wire rack in your Power Pressure Cooker XL; pour in 2 cups of water. Lower the ramekins onto the rack. Place the lid on the Power Pressure Cooker XL, lock the lid and switch the pressure release valve to closed.
6. Cook for 12 minutes. Once the timer reaches 0, the cooker will automatically switch to "KEEP WARM/ CANCEL". Switch the pressure release valve to open.
7. When the steam is completely released, remove the lid. Serve well chilled.

137. Dark Chocolate Cake

This comforting childhood classic is super-simple and perfect for any occasion. Many studies have proven that dark chocolate can positively affect your health.

Servings 6

Ready in about 20 minutes

NUTRITIONAL INFORMATION (Per Serving)

464 - Calories
27.1g - Fat
50.3g - Carbs
6.3g - Protein
40.4g - Sugars

Ingredients

- 1/3 cup white flour
- 1 cup sugar
- 2 cups dark chocolate
- 1/2 cup butter, softened
- 1/2 teaspoon hazelnut extract
- 1/2 teaspoon cinnamon powder
- 1 teaspoon vanilla extract
- 4 small-sized eggs

Directions

1. Press the "CHICKEN/MEAT" key. Press the "TIME ADJUSTMENT" key and set the timer for 10 minutes.
2. Prepare the Power Pressure Cooker XL by adding 1 cup of water and a wire rack to the inner pot.
3. Microwave the chocolate with the butter for 1 to 2 minutes. Add the other ingredients and beat with an electric mixer.
4. Divide the prepared batter among six ramekins; lower the ramekins onto the rack.
5. Place the lid on the Power Pressure Cooker XL, lock the lid and switch the pressure release valve to closed.
6. Press the "CANCEL" key. Switch the pressure release valve to open. When the steam is completely released, remove the cooker's lid.
7. Let them cool on a rack before serving. Bon appétit!

138. Coconut-Vanilla Custard

When you find yourself wanting to reach for something sweet, try this flavorful custard that will please everyone. Rediscover the pleasure of making homemade desserts!

Servings 8

Ready in about 25 minutes

NUTRITIONAL INFORMATION
(Per Serving)

252 - Calories
22.7g - Fat
6.8g - Carbs
8.1g - Protein
4.9g - Sugars

Ingredients

- 1 ½ cups water
- 2 ½ cups canned coconut milk
- 1 ½ cups milk
- 1 teaspoon coconut extract
- 1/2 teaspoon pure vanilla extract
- 4 whole eggs plus 4 egg yolks, lightly beaten

Directions

1. Press the "SOUP/STEW" key.
2. Pour the regular milk and coconut milk into a sauté pan; bring to a boil over a medium-high flame.
3. In a separate bowl, mix the egg and egg yolks. Next, add 2 tablespoons of the warm milk mixture to the whisked egg mixture.
4. Then, add the vanilla extract and coconut extract; mix until everything is well combined.
5. Transfer the mixture to the simmering milk and stir to combine. Continue simmering for about 4 minutes, stirring continuously to prevent burning.
6. Next, lightly grease a 6-cup soufflé pan; pour the mixture into the soufflé pan. Cover with foil.
7. Add the water and wire rack to the Power Pressure Cooker XL; place the soufflé dish on the wire rack.
8. Place the lid on the Power Pressure Cooker XL, lock the lid and switch the pressure release valve to closed.
9. Cook for 20 minutes. Once the timer reaches 0, the cooker will automatically switch to "KEEP WARM/ CANCEL". Switch the pressure release valve to open. When the steam is completely released, remove the lid.
10. Garnish with coconut flakes. Bon appétit!

139. Apple and Fig Oatmeal Crisp

Looking for an easy dessert to seal the end of a meal? An oatmeal crisp is a great choice! Did you know that dried figs improve reproductive health and digestion?

Servings 6

Ready in about 20 minutes

NUTRITIONAL INFORMATION (Per Serving)

305 - Calories
16.5g - Fat
38.4g - Carbs
3.4g - Protein
19.9g - Sugars

Ingredients

- 1 stick butter
- 1/2 cup dried figs, chopped
- 1/3 cup flour
- 1/2 teaspoon ground cloves
- 1/2 teaspoon pure vanilla extract
- 1/3 cup brown sugar
- 1/4 teaspoon cinnamon powder
- 1/4 teaspoon grated nutmeg
- 1 cup old-fashioned oats
- 1 pound apples, cored, peeled and sliced
- 1 ½ cups warm water

Directions

1. Choose the "RICE/RISOTTO" function. Press the "TIME ADJUSTMENT" key and set the time to 12 minutes.
2. Combine the oats, flour, brown sugar, vanilla, nutmeg, ground cloves, cinnamon powder, and the butter. Arrange the sliced apples on the bottom of a lightly-buttered baking dish.
3. Spread the oat crisp mixture over the apples. Top with chopped figs. Cover the baking dish with foil. Add the warm water to the inner pot of your Power Pressure Cooker XL.
4. Place the wire rack in the Power Pressure Cooker XL. Lower the baking dish onto the wire rack.
5. Place the lid on the Power Pressure Cooker XL, lock the lid and switch the pressure release valve to closed.
6. Once the timer reaches 0, the cooker will automatically switch to "KEEP WARM/CANCEL". Switch the pressure release valve to open. When the steam is completely released, remove the lid. Enjoy!

140. Pecan and Pumpkin Pie Pudding

Pumpkin is fall's unavoidable ingredient. Apart from being rich in fiber, pumpkin is vitamin-packed food. Enjoy!

Servings 4

Ready in about 30 minutes

NUTRITIONAL INFORMATION (Per Serving)

470 - Calories
34.8g - Fat
34.4g - Carbs
9.4g - Protein
21.3g - Sugars

Ingredients

- Nonstick cooking spray
- 1 tablespoon flour
- 1/2 teaspoon vanilla essence
- 1/2 teaspoon ground cloves
- 3 eggs, at room temperature
- 1/2 teaspoon ground cinnamon
- 1/3 cup dark brown sugar
- 1/2 cup toasted pecans, for garnish
- 1 cup heavy cream
- 2 cups canned pumpkin
- 1 ½ tablespoons molasses

Directions

1. Press the "CHICKEN/MEAT" key. Lightly grease the bottom and sides of a round soufflé dish with a nonstick cooking spray; set aside.
2. Combine the canned pumpkin, brown sugar, heavy cream, eggs, molasses, and vanilla essence in a large bowl. Whisk in the flour, cloves, and cinnamon.
3. Pour the mixture into the prepared soufflé dish. Cover with foil.
4. Add the wire rack and 2 cups of water to the Power Pressure Cooker XL. Create an aluminum foil sling.
5. Place the lid on the Power Pressure Cooker XL, lock the lid and switch the pressure release valve to closed. Cook for 20 minutes.
6. Once the timer reaches 0, the cooker will automatically switch to "KEEP WARM/CANCEL". Switch the pressure release valve to open.
7. When the steam is completely released, remove the lid. Serve with toasted pecans.

141. Challah Bread Pudding with Nuts

If you're not a fan of nutmeg – just leave it out of this recipe! You can use ground cinnamon, vanilla, anise star and even ground allspice instead.

Servings 6

Ready in about 25 minutes

NUTRITIONAL INFORMATION (Per Serving)

413 - Calories
24.7g - Fat
36.4g - Carbs
11.5g - Protein
21.5g - Sugars

Ingredients

- 1 stick butter
- 1/8 teaspoon grated nutmeg
- 3 tablespoons hazelnuts, chopped
- 1 tablespoon almonds, chopped
- 1/2 cup sugar
- 1 ½ cups water
- 3 whole eggs plus 3 egg yolks
- 1 ½ tablespoons rum
- 1 teaspoon hazelnut extract
- 1/4 teaspoon salt
- 1/2 tablespoon honey
- 3 cups Challah, torn into bite-sized pieces
- 1 ½ cups milk

Directions

1. Press the "RICO/RISOTTO" key. Simply add the Challah to a lightly greased baking dish. Then, make the custard by mixing all the remaining ingredients.
2. Pour the custard mixture over the Challah pieces. Cover with an aluminum foil.
3. Insert the wire rack in the inner pot of your Power Pressure Cooker XL. Pour in 2 cups of water.
4. Place the lid on the Power Pressure Cooker XL, lock the lid and switch the pressure release valve to closed. Cook for 20 minutes.
5. Afterwards, perform a Natural pressure release. Serve at room temperature.

142. Cashew Chocolate Cake

You can easily make your own nut meal (nut flour) in a food processor or blender. You can even utilize a coffee grinder just like grandma used to make.

Servings 10

Ready in about 50 minutes

NUTRITIONAL INFORMATION (Per Serving)

522 - Calories
31.7g - Fat
58.3g - Carbs
6.9g - Protein
47.7g - Sugars

Ingredients

For the Crust:
- 2 cups nut meal
- 1/3 cup coconut oil, room temperature
- 1/3 cup brown sugar

For the Filling:
- 1/4 teaspoon grated nutmeg
- 1 cup chocolate chips
- 1/2 teaspoon cinnamon powder
- 1/2 teaspoon vanilla essence
- 2 cups cashews, chopped, soaked and drained
- 1/2 cup sugar
- 3/4 cup coconut milk

Directions

1. Press the "CHICKEN/MEAT" key. Combine all the ingredients for the crust. Press the crust mixture into a silicone cake pan. You can use the back of a spoon; transfer the crust to a refrigerator.
2. Then, make the filling by mixing all the filling ingredients. Pour the filling over the crust.
3. Put the wire rack into the Power Pressure Cooker XL. Now, lower the cake pan onto the rack.
4. Place the lid on the Power Pressure Cooker XL, lock the lid and switch the pressure release valve to closed. Cook for 45 minutes.
5. Once the timer reaches 0, the cooker will automatically switch to "KEEP WARM/CANCEL". Switch the pressure release valve to open.
6. When the steam is completely released, remove the lid. Serve well chilled.

143. Nana's Walnut Zucchini Bread

Here's an old-fashioned recipe that is actually lip-smacking good! Add a festive look to your dessert table every day with this rich and delectable zucchini bread.

Servings 10

Ready in about 35 minutes

NUTRITIONAL INFORMATION (Per Serving)

447 - Calories
19.6g - Fat
63.8g - Carbs
8.9g - Protein
36.9g - Sugars

Ingredients

- 1/3 cup walnuts, chopped
- 1 cup chocolate chips
- 1 stick butter, at room temperature
- 1/4 teaspoon cinnamon powder
- 1 1/3 cups sugar
- 2 ¼ cups all-purpose flour
- 1 teaspoon baking soda
- 1 teaspoon hazelnut extract
- 1/2 teaspoon vanilla extract
- 1/3 teaspoon baking powder
- 1/3 cup applesauce
- 4 eggs
- 3/4 cup cocoa powder
- 1 ½ cups zucchini, peeled and grated

Directions

1. Press the "CHICKEN/MEAT" key. In a mixing dish, combine the eggs, butter, applesauce, sugar, hazelnut extract, and vanilla extract. Add in the zucchini and stir to combine.
2. In a separate mixing dish, combine the other items. Stir in the egg-zucchini mixture and mix to combine well.
3. Put the wire rack into the inner pot of the Power Pressure Cooker XL; pour in 1 ½ cups water. Pour the batter into a lightly greased baking pan that will fit your Power Pressure Cooker XL. Place the baking pan on the wire rack.
4. Place the lid on the Power Pressure Cooker XL, lock the lid and switch the pressure release valve to closed. Cook for 30 minutes.
5. Once the timer reaches 0, the cooker will automatically switch to "KEEP WARM/CANCEL". Switch the pressure release valve to open.
6. When the steam is completely released, remove the lid. Lastly, allow the cake to cool before serving.

144. Delectable Honey and Walnut Dessert

Honey and walnut are paired with rice for a great, light ending to your meal. This pudding tastes absolutely divine!

Servings 6

Ready in about 25 minutes

NUTRITIONAL
INFORMATION
(Per Serving)

440 - Calories
5.8g - Fat
90.8g - Carbs
8.8g - Protein
33g - Sugars

Ingredients

- 3 ripe bananas, mashed
- 1/8 teaspoon ground cloves
- 2 cups basmati rice
- 1/3 cup walnuts, ground
- 1/2 cup honey
- 1 tablespoon candied ginger, diced
- 1/4 teaspoon ground cinnamon
- 2 ½ cups water
- 1 ½ cups soy milk

Directions

1. Press the "RICO/RISOTTO" key. Simply combine all the ingredients in your Power Pressure Cooker XL; stir until everything is well combined.
2. Place the lid on the Power Pressure Cooker XL, lock the lid and switch the pressure release valve to closed. Cook for 15 minutes.
3. Once the timer reaches 0, the cooker will automatically switch to "KEEP WARM/CANCEL". Switch the pressure release valve to open.
4. When the steam is completely released, remove the lid. Serve in individual bowls. Bon appétit!

145. The Best Apple Crisp Ever

Inspired by crispy apples, you can come up with this dessert idea that's so easy and literally scrumptious! Serve with a dollop of vanilla ice cream and enjoy!

Servings 4

Ready in about 25 minutes

NUTRITIONAL INFORMATION (Per Serving)

429 - Calories
24.8g - Fat
50.5g - Carbs
4.6g - Protein
23.2g - Sugars

Ingredients

- 1 ½ cups warm water
- 1 cup old-fashioned oats
- 1/2 teaspoon lemon rind, grated
- 1/8 teaspoon sea salt
- 1 teaspoon ground cinnamon
- 1/3 cup sugar
- 1/2 teaspoon grated nutmeg
- 1/2 cup flour
- 1 stick butter, softened
- 1/2 tablespoon lemon juice
- 1 pound Granny Smith apples, cored, peeled and thinly sliced

Directions

1. Press the "RICO/RISOTTO" key. Sprinkle the apples with lemon juice.
2. In another bowl, mix the lemon rind, oats, flour, sugar, nutmeg, cinnamon, salt, and butter. Next, layer the apples and the crisp mixture in a baking dish, ending with the layer of crisp mixture. Cover the dish with foil.
3. Add the wire rack and warm water to the inner pot of the Power Pressure Cooker XL. Place the baking dish on the rack.
4. Place the lid on the Power Pressure Cooker XL, lock the lid and switch the pressure release valve to closed. Cook for 20 minutes.
5. Once the timer reaches 0, the cooker will automatically switch to "KEEP WARM/CANCEL". Switch the pressure release valve to open.
6. When the steam is completely released, remove the lid. Bon appétit!

146. Summer Apricot and Coconut Delight

Looking for an easy and satisfying dessert? This fragrant and nutritious concoction will be the perfect answer to what your tummy desire!

Servings 6

Ready in about 25 minutes

NUTRITIONAL INFORMATION (Per Serving)

504 - Calories
28.5g - Fat
58.6g - Carbs
7.1g - Protein
6.5g - Sugars

Ingredients

- 2 cups jasmine rice
- 1 cup ripe apricots, pitted and halved
- 1 tablespoon candied ginger, diced
- 1 teaspoon orange zest
- 1/4 teaspoon vanilla extract
- 2 ½ cups coconut milk
- 1 ½ cups water
- 1 cup shredded coconut

Directions

1. Press the "RICO/RISOTTO" key. Simply add all of the above ingredients to your Power Pressure Cooker XL.
2. Place the lid on the Power Pressure Cooker XL, lock the lid and switch the pressure release valve to closed. Cook for 18 minutes.
3. Once the timer reaches 0, the cooker will automatically switch to "KEEP WARM/CANCEL". Switch the pressure release valve to open.
4. When the steam is completely released, remove the lid. Serve well-chilled. Bon appétit!

147. Aromatic Pears in Red Wine Sauce

Want to impress your guests at your next dinner party?
Wow them with this classic dessert with a new twist.

Servings 6

Ready in about 15 minutes

NUTRITIONAL INFORMATION (Per Serving)

317 - Calories
1.3g - Fat
70.9g - Carbs
1.4g - Protein
62.4g - Sugars

Ingredients

- 1 ½ pounds pears, peeled
- 1 ¼ cups red wine
- 2 vanilla beans
- 10 ounces caster sugar
- 2 cloves
- 2 cinnamon sticks

Directions

1. Press the "SOUP/STEW" key. Add all of the above ingredients to the Power Pressure Cooker XL.
2. Place the lid on the Power Pressure Cooker XL, lock the lid and switch the pressure release valve to closed. Cook for 10 minutes.
3. Once the timer reaches 0, the cooker will automatically switch to "KEEP WARM/CANCEL". Switch the pressure release valve to open.
4. When the steam is completely released, remove the lid. Bon appétit!

148. Quick and Easy Stuffed Apples

These stuffed apples will remind you of your childhood!
Serve with a generous portion of vanilla ice cream for a
great presentation!

Servings 4

Ready in about
20 minutes

**NUTRITIONAL
INFORMATION**
(Per Serving)

381 - Calories
22.5g - Fat
38.6g - Carbs
6.9g - Protein
0.4g - Sugars

Ingredients

- 1 ½ cups water
- 1/2 stick butter, softened
- 1/2 tablespoon lemon zest, grated
- 1 teaspoon vanilla paste
- 1/4 cup walnuts, chopped
- 6 apples, cored and halved
- 10 cinnamon cookies, crumbled

Directions

1. Press the "RICE/RISOTTO" key. Prepare the Power Pressure Cooker XL by adding 1 ½ cups of warm water and the wire rack.
2. In a mixing bowl, combine the walnuts, cookie crumbs, lemon zest, and vanilla paste. Stuff the apples; transfer the apples to the wire rack; dot with the softened butter.
3. Place the lid on the Power Pressure Cooker XL, lock the lid and switch the pressure release valve to closed. Cook for 15 minutes.
4. Once the timer reaches 0, the cooker will automatically switch to "KEEP WARM/CANCEL". Switch the pressure release valve to open.
5. When the steam is completely released, remove the lid. Serve at room temperature.

149. Gorgeous Crème Brule

~

Here's a gorgeous family dessert that is served in individual bowls. It only takes a few minutes to whip up the ingredients and less than 10 minutes to cook everything in the Power Pressure Cooker XL. Lovely!

Servings 4

Ready in about
20 minutes
+ chilling time

NUTRITIONAL
INFORMATION
(Per Serving)

430 - Calories
11.6g - Fat
64.2g - Carbs
2.9g - Protein
62.6g - Sugars

Ingredients

- 1 ¼ cups warm water
- 1/2 teaspoon vanilla paste
- 1 ½ cups warm heavy cream
- 3 large-sized egg yolks, large
- 1 cup sugar
- 1/4 cup granulated sugar

Directions

1. Press the "SOUP/STEW" key.
2. Mix the heavy cream, sugar, vanilla, and the egg yolks in a bowl. Then, fill four ramekins with this mixture and wrap them with foil.
3. Pour the warm water into the inner pot of the Power Pressure Cooker XL. Add the wire rack; arrange the ramekins on the rack.
4. Place the lid on the Power Pressure Cooker XL, lock the lid and switch the pressure release valve to closed. Cook for 10 minutes.
5. Once the timer reaches 0, the cooker will automatically switch to "KEEP WARM/CANCEL". Switch the pressure release valve to open.
6. When the steam is completely released, remove the lid. Next, refrigerate your Crème Brule for at least 3 hours.
7. Top with the granulated sugar; to caramelize the sugar, place the ramekins under the broiler. Enjoy!

150. White Chocolate Lemon Pudding

Creamy and delicious, this lemon pudding is a true comfort in a bowl! To serve, you can drizzle individual portions with white chocolate glaze.

Servings 6

Ready in about 20 minutes

NUTRITIONAL INFORMATION (Per Serving)

399 - Calories
29.5g - Fat
29.9g - Carbs
5.6g - Protein
26.5g - Sugars

Ingredients

- 3 egg yolks, whisked
- 1 ¼ cups heavy cream
- 1 ¼ cups half-and-half
- 1 teaspoon grated ginger
- 1/2 tablespoon finely grated lemon zest
- 2 tablespoons sugar
- 8 ounces white chocolate, chopped
- 1/2 teaspoon lemon extract

Directions

1. Press the "SOUP/STEW" key.
2. Put the white chocolate into a large-sized mixing dish. Combine the cream and half-and-half in a saucepan and warm over medium-low heat.
3. Pour the warm cream mixture over the white chocolate; whisk until everything is melted. Add the remaining ingredients and whisk to combine.
4. Pour the mixture into six heat-safe ramekins; cover each ramekin with foil. Add the wire rack and 2 cups water to the Power Pressure Cooker XL.
5. Lower the ramekins onto the rack. Place the lid on the Power Pressure Cooker XL, lock the lid and switch the pressure release valve to closed.
6. Cook for 13 minutes. Once the timer reaches 0, the cooker will automatically switch to "KEEP WARM/ CANCEL". Switch the pressure release valve to open. When the steam is completely released, remove the lid. Bon appétit!

1. Potato and Wheat Berry Breakfast

Did you know that wheat berries don't require an overnight soak? You can do that, but if you are in a hurry, boil them for 1 hour before pressure cooking.

Servings 4

Ready in about 20 minutes

NUTRITIONAL INFORMATION (Per Serving)

371 - Calories
7.3g - Fat
70.1g - Carbs
10.9g - Protein
2.2g - Sugars

Ingredients

- 5 teaspoons sesame oil
- 3 cloves garlic, smashed
- 1 medium-sized leek, peeled and sliced
- 7 cups water
- 2 ¼ cups white wheat berries, soaked overnight
- 5 medium-sized potatoes, cubed
- 1/4 teaspoon ground black pepper, or more to taste
- 1 teaspoon seasoned salt
- 1 teaspoon dried thyme

Directions

1. Combine the white wheat berries with water in your Instant Pot.
2. In a medium-sized skillet, warm the sesame oil over medium-high flame. Then, sauté the leeks and garlic until tender. Stir in the thyme; cook for 1 more minute, stirring a few times.
3. Choose "Multi-grain" function; cook your wheat together with potatoes for about 20 minutes.
4. When the mixture is ready, add sautéed leeks with garlic.
5. Sprinkle with seasoned salt and black pepper to taste. Serve.

1. Potato and Wheat Berry Breakfast

Did you know that wheat berries don't require an overnight soak? You can do that, but if you are in a hurry, boil them for 1 hour before pressure cooking.

Servings 4

Ready in about 20 minutes

NUTRITIONAL INFORMATION (Per Serving)

371 - Calories
7.3g - Fat
70.1g - Carbs
10.9g - Protein
2.2g - Sugars

Ingredients

- 5 teaspoons sesame oil
- 3 cloves garlic, smashed
- 1 medium-sized leek, peeled and sliced
- 7 cups water
- 2 ¼ cups white wheat berries, soaked overnight
- 5 medium-sized potatoes, cubed
- 1/4 teaspoon ground black pepper, or more to taste
- 1 teaspoon seasoned salt
- 1 teaspoon dried thyme

Directions

1. Combine the white wheat berries with water in your Instant Pot.
2. In a medium-sized skillet, warm the sesame oil over medium-high flame. Then, sauté the leeks and garlic until tender. Stir in the thyme; cook for 1 more minute, stirring a few times.
3. Choose "Multi-grain" function; cook your wheat together with potatoes for about 20 minutes.
4. When the mixture is ready, add sautéed leeks with garlic.
5. Sprinkle with seasoned salt and black pepper to taste. Serve.

1. Potato and Wheat Berry Breakfast

Did you know that wheat berries don't require an overnight soak? You can do that, but if you are in a hurry, boil them for 1 hour before pressure cooking.

Servings 4

Ready in about 20 minutes

NUTRITIONAL INFORMATION (Per Serving)

371 - Calories
7.3g - Fat
70.1g - Carbs
10.9g - Protein
2.2g - Sugars

Ingredients

- 5 teaspoons sesame oil
- 3 cloves garlic, smashed
- 1 medium-sized leek, peeled and sliced
- 7 cups water
- 2 ¼ cups white wheat berries, soaked overnight
- 5 medium-sized potatoes, cubed
- 1/4 teaspoon ground black pepper, or more to taste
- 1 teaspoon seasoned salt
- 1 teaspoon dried thyme

Directions

1. Combine the white wheat berries with water in your Instant Pot.
2. In a medium-sized skillet, warm the sesame oil over medium-high flame. Then, sauté the leeks and garlic until tender. Stir in the thyme; cook for 1 more minute, stirring a few times.
3. Choose "Multi-grain" function; cook your wheat together with potatoes for about 20 minutes.
4. When the mixture is ready, add sautéed leeks with garlic.
5. Sprinkle with seasoned salt and black pepper to taste. Serve.

1. Potato and Wheat Berry Breakfast

Did you know that wheat berries don't require an overnight soak? You can do that, but if you are in a hurry, boil them for 1 hour before pressure cooking.

Servings 4

Ready in about 20 minutes

NUTRITIONAL INFORMATION (Per Serving)

371 - Calories
7.3g - Fat
70.1g - Carbs
10.9g - Protein
2.2g - Sugars

Ingredients

- 5 teaspoons sesame oil
- 3 cloves garlic, smashed
- 1 medium-sized leek, peeled and sliced
- 7 cups water
- 2 ¼ cups white wheat berries, soaked overnight
- 5 medium-sized potatoes, cubed
- 1/4 teaspoon ground black pepper, or more to taste
- 1 teaspoon seasoned salt
- 1 teaspoon dried thyme

Directions

1. Combine the white wheat berries with water in your Instant Pot.
2. In a medium-sized skillet, warm the sesame oil over medium-high flame. Then, sauté the leeks and garlic until tender. Stir in the thyme; cook for 1 more minute, stirring a few times.
3. Choose "Multi-grain" function; cook your wheat together with potatoes for about 20 minutes.
4. When the mixture is ready, add sautéed leeks with garlic.
5. Sprinkle with seasoned salt and black pepper to taste. Serve.

Made in the USA
Lexington, KY
12 July 2017